Help! I'm Married to the PASTOR

Learning to Love Your Life of Ministry

Kimberly Waldie

Help! I'm Married to the Pastor – Learning to Love Your Life of Ministry

ISBN 978-0-9969568-1-9

Table of Contents

Acknowledgements

There are many people who helped in the preparation of this book. First, I would like to thank my church family, Living Hope Church, for their patience, love, and support of us along our ministry journey. I can truly say that loving and leading them has been one of the greatest privileges of my life. I didn't always get it right in ministry but they have never held it against me. I can't wait to see what awaits us in heaven when all that God has touched through this faithful congregation in Traverse City, MI is revealed.

A great big thank-you goes out to Anthony Weber, Hannah Thelander, and Jaime Hlavin, who helped in critiquing, editing, and offering feedback in the writing of this book. I am amazed how many different ways a person can say the same thing. Your suggestions and thoughtful insight was profoundly helpful.

I am forever grateful to my designer and creative friend, Dee-Dee Franklin. Everything you touch becomes more beautiful. This is true in every part of your life. Your ability to take something and break it down into manageable pieces is a wonderful gift. I am so thankful to have walked this journey with you.

Last, but certainly not least, my deepest thanks goes to my family. To my husband, Carey, who is my greatest coach, fan, and best friend, for his constant ability to inspire me to do hard things and cheer me on. Your support to get this job done and express in words what I was feeling in my heart for people who are called to a life to ministry was priceless. To our children, Cal, Madison, A.J., and Mikayla–you make each day an adventure and I wouldn't be the woman I am today but for the privilege of raising each of you. Thanks for always encouraging me to keep going. I can't wait to see what God does with the seeds sown in your lives.

Introduction

There are so many reasons why I wrote this book. I wrote because I've grown over the years to love my ministry life and to love pastor's wives. I wrote because I know how hard the enemy works to convince them that they are a mistake. I want each one to know that she is a purposeful part of God's redemptive story and she can find joy in the journey and in the serving.

I wrote because I love our congregations–filled with so many different people–who seek to get this business of following Jesus right. I want to see them mature and enjoy the adventure of serving Jesus.

But more than anything, I've grown to appreciate the privilege and opportunity we have as ministers to represent Jesus to those same people in some of the most important moments of their lives. We are there at the birth or the wedding. We are there to answer the phone in the middle of the night when trouble strikes. Yes, it's exhausting. Yes, it's difficult at times. However, I'm convinced more than ever that all of these sacrifices are worth it. I'm convinced that God doesn't miss a single thing that is offered up to Him in love, sweat, and prayer. I'm convinced that He is faithful to take those seeds and do things that will last long after all of us are gone. It is His story after all. I want us to do things together that will last forever.

One more thing. We need each other to get the job of making sure *every* person has a chance to know Jesus finished. If one of us quits, there is a loss to the body of Christ. So don't quit, my friend. No matter what comes, Jesus is worthy of your sacrificed life. Embrace the opportunity that God has given you. Trust that God will give you everything you need for each divine moment as it comes and learn to love your life of ministry.

Chapter 1

Help! What Was I Thinking?

My mind races as I struggle to put the words on paper, *"What was I ever thinking going into ministry?"*

Have you ever asked yourself this question? It feels so long ago that my husband and I began this journey to the place we are today. Over twenty years of ministry and life have gone by. Marriage, youth groups, children, jobs, Bible studies, more children, more jobs, too many small groups to count, and sermons—so many sermons preached to so many different people. Looking at my life today, here in my comfortable Lazy-boy snuggled up next to the fireplace with a cup of coffee and my Bible, you would never imagine the discomfort that has been my companion so many times during this journey. In fact, I still can't believe God chose me to do this.

On second thought, what was HE thinking?

It's easy to look at the outward appearance of other people and think how *"put-together"* they are, how they must have walked into life and ministry with all their ducks in row. But rarely does that happen. Rather, most of us find our journey with Christ and into ministry difficult, dirty, less than glamorous, and yes, sometimes even painful. It is through those times of difficulty and pain that God brings growth and maturity. It forces us to a place of obedience—or not. But it is always our choice.

My guess is that because you are reading this book, you, too, have chosen to walk into a life of ministry, or are seriously considering this option. God has already made His choice to provide us with the opportunity to answer His call. He believes we can do it with His help. Here I am, and here you are, sitting in this place writing or reading because He has called us. What we do or don't do with it is our responsibility.

Why Am I Here?

My story is probably not all that different from your story. There was nothing spectacular, or hugely defining, in my life to indicate I was prepared or qualified for the life of a pastor's wife. In fact, there were probably more red flags for why I shouldn't be in ministry. That sounds a lot like God, doesn't it?

Growing up actively involved in the church, I found myself immersed in a world where all of my life seemed to revolve around a church setting. Perhaps that was God's way of preparing me for ministry. Perhaps it was simply grace. Either one is fine with me. My parents dragged me to church three times a week regardless of my physical state. If I was sick it was a great opportunity to *"go, and get prayed for."* I can't tell you how many times I heard those words spoken to me. I still cringe when I hear them today.

We went to school, but our social activities at school or in the neighborhood were minimal. Our lives were about being at church with our church family. My parents encouraged good grades but rarely did they encourage or allow outside activity that was not church-related. I'm not sure of the reason. Maybe it was just what everyone else in our church did. Our life and church obligations were the top priority. I realize now that this is a foreign philosophy for many church people in today's world. Instead, we find now that we live in a culture that compartmentalizes church to a weekly activity where we show up, hear a great message (hopefully), and go home to live our lives—too many times unchanged. Jesus is a counselor or advisor, but rarely is He allowed to be relevant in all areas of our lives. My goal is to find and keep the balance between these two extremes for my children. It's not always an easy task, but it's my goal, nonetheless.

Back to those early years: I was probably the irritating little girl in children's church who liked to have all the right answers. I was an excellent student who loved reading, but I was also a perfectionist from the start and fearful of everything, especially people. As a shy, introverted girl, it felt good to receive attention and affirmation when I succeeded. So whatever I was allowed to do,

I would try my best to do it well. Halfway through grade school, my grades at school were so high that the school approached my parents about double-promoting me from fourth grade to sixth grade.

This was a move, in hindsight, that for me created more trouble than good. Not only did I miss sex education, which was offered in fifth grade (and left me completely uninformed), but this shy, introverted child moved up to a new peer group the year before junior high, the "old school" version of middle school. I don't recommend it to parents today. It was troubling socially. I had few friends and very little capacity—or opportunity—for making new friends, before the awful years of junior high were upon me. Insecure and intimidated, I turned inwardly to my studies and put my head down. No one asked me how I was doing, and I can't remember ever thinking of telling someone how I felt. It was just misery.

Early on, I learned to dislike disappointing people. I preferred, like most people, to have positive attention and affirmation. It was less conflicting, and it felt less like disappointing. It is strange because it was never communicated to me that I was disappointing anyone. My parents never acted disappointed in me but for some reason, I really struggled hard to make sure I pleased the people around me. It was better to stay silent rather than let others down. *(My husband and kids find this one hard to believe today.)* Since this became the trend for my life early on, it would be many years before I would fully understand just how much this coping mechanism impacted my heart, especially in ministry. Fear of disappointing and the struggles of perfectionism create great insecurities for a pastor's wife, or for anyone. Even now I battle those old insecurities when they rise to the surface. It can be an enslaving trait to carry into ministry.

Loving His Word

In seventh grade, my youth pastor convinced me to join the Senior (now called Teen) Bible Quiz team at my church. This was an open door to camaraderie and purpose for a twelve-year old girl who was struggling socially. It put my perfectionism to work and gave me a place where I was socially accepted. For those who are unfamiliar with Bible Quiz, each year the teams focused on one book of the Bible (or set of smaller books). They studied and competed over the content and memorization of that particular book.

At the same time I joined the team, another young man also joined. He was a smart kid with a capacity to memorize that would make any Hollywood actor envious. He was shy and awkward like me, but his capacity for memorizing was phenomenal. Together with a few other kids, we formed a team that over the years became a winning combination at our state, region, and eventually, at the national level. Overall, I left my Bible Quiz career with thirteen books of the Bible memorized, five state championships, two regional championships, one national championship (1985 San Antonio, Texas) plus many more 'tournament' wins. I also found I had grown from a shy, introverted little girl to an assertive, competitive, and skilled competitor. My teammate and I shared the top honors individually wherever we competed.

In that season of my life, I had no desire and felt no call to be in ministry. In fact, I was really struggling in my walk with Christ. Though life had been about church, it really wasn't about knowing Jesus and developing an intimate relationship with Him. I fear this is a great danger for the church kid. It's so easy to go through the motions of religion in our church worlds without ever encountering Christ. We can believe we have it all together, but our hearts are far from Him. That's where I was when I graduated from high school. Though I was heading to Bible college on a Bible Quiz scholarship, it was only for the scholarship. My heart wasn't interested in anything else. Isn't it wonderful that God knows us better than we know ourselves? As we look over the tapestry of our lives, we are usually humbled. Even when we are motivated by the wrong things, God is still working in our lives to lead us down the right path. Even when we see ourselves under the light of intimidation and unworthiness, He shines the light on our inherent value and potential in Christ.

Bible Quiz taught me something beautiful much later in life, and something totally unexpected that I wouldn't have understood during those exciting moments of competition. As I look back over the journey, I am so thankful for the preparation that studying and memorizing the Word of God gave me for life, not only as a pastor's wife, but as a follower of Christ. I could not, as a young teen, comprehend how unimportant those awards, medals, and championships would be, compared to having the Word buried deep in my heart. It is the Word that has carried me through the difficult and painful times in my life. It is the Word that has laid the personal foundation for understanding my identity in Christ and helped me overcome the intimidation that ministry brings all of us. It was (and still is) the Word poured deep into my heart that was my daily guide as I learned to teach, exhort, and disciple others in their own faith journeys.

How Did You Get Here?

So what were YOU thinking by going into ministry? I know you have a story. We all do. You may not have grown up in church. In fact, you may not have even had the benefit of living in a family that followed Jesus. You may not have memorized thirteen books of the Bible. None of that matters. None of those things qualify you to serve in ministry anyway. It's so easy to look at your story and fall victim to the intimidation of the enemy. Intimidation that says you shouldn't be the pastor's wife. And that is just what he would like you to believe. Even if you do decide to serve, he would like nothing better than to have you live under a shroud of unworthiness and insecurity. It keeps you trapped and eventually will find you resentful of the role that you're in today. So that's why I wrote this book. I wrote it for you. I want you to realize that you can let go of all the reasons why you shouldn't be a pastor's wife, embrace all the reasons that God chose you, and through it all learn to genuinely love your life. It is really our willingness to serve and love both Christ and His Bride that truly qualifies us to be in ministry. Sounds a bit ridiculous, doesn't it? If I were doing the choosing, I would pick someone else besides me. Wouldn't the Body of Christ be better served by people who dreamed of a life of ministry, were articulate and stage-perfect, or had multiple theology degrees? Maybe, or maybe not.

When God asks us to serve, He isn't checking our resume, at least not a resume that follows the qualifications of the world. Those things don't impress Him much anyway. He knows that what you will need to serve the church on this journey is found only in Him. Obviously, you will need to grow your skills, learn the Word, and develop good disciplines. However, the real fruit in ministry comes from the empowerment of His Spirit. We cannot transform a heart. We can move people emotionally with our words or music, but real and lasting transformation is something only He can do. That seems to put all of us on an even playing field, since He is the One who qualifies those He calls. I have learned over the years to be leery of those entering ministry who presume they are well-qualified or walk in pride. They may have a rough ride down the path of humility.

While there are a few people who may dream about being in ministry, more of us seem to find ministry thrust upon us. Maybe that's how it happened to you. Perhaps you weren't even asked. I know women just like you who feel like the title of pastor's wife was an unfair assignment they didn't want. As a result, the title brings a great deal of intimidation and feels like a heavy burden.

Can I encourage you today? It was no mistake. It is no mistake. While our thoughts early on may have never been ministry-focused, God has been thinking about you since before you were born. He has brought you to this place of ministry to make you into a beautiful picture of His Son, and to help you make others beautiful as well. Yes, there will be times of difficulty. There will be seasons of great growth. There will be disappointments and unfortunately, even pain. But when you rest in that foundation of truth that God is not surprised by your new (or old) place of ministry and has been preparing you for this moment (and all future moments) all your life, you can be at peace. Peace to no longer wrestle against His call. Peace to realize you are exactly where He thought you would be. For many of my early ministry years, I found myself reacting like Moses; I was always arguing with God that there must be someone better who could do my job. Maybe you, too, understand this resistance. Then something happened in my stubborn heart.

As I grew in my relationship with Him, I realized what a waste of time it is to argue with God over my place as a pastor's wife. This is true for two reasons. First, He knows what we need in our lives to sharpen us into the daughters He wants us to be. We can't think like He can. We can't dream like He can. So it's important to trust Him.

Secondly, there is a real shortage of authentic and committed Christ-followers willing to care for His Bride. Not perfect men and women. Not charismatic "pretty-people" who do it all perfectly. But real people who are authentic in their walk with Christ. There aren't enough people who are willing to give up their personal comforts and personal privacy to commit themselves to serve Christ in every aspect of life. There aren't enough people who are committed to being more like Christ, and less like themselves. People who are committed to helping others know Him, too. God wants you on the team so He can refine and sharpen you. We need you on the team to lead the body of Christ more effectively. Together we can make a difference. You don't need to battle the high bar of perfection any longer. It was many years into my ministry life that I discovered God wasn't holding that bar of perfection anyway. The bar was, unfortunately, being held up by me. You don't need to continually struggle under the weight of how you fall short. If this wasn't your first choice in life, allow God the freedom to grow you, so you can finally learn to love being on the ministry team!

It is a privilege to serve Christ as a pastor's wife. It is an honor to represent Him and love His sheep. You aren't in ministry because you are "qualified." You are in this place because He saw you, and in His grace, He saved you from the death penalty of your sin. He wanted to be reconciled to you so desperately that He chose to die for you. He chose to die so that you could live. That's why I'm here, too. He wants to use the testimony of that grace in all of us to free others. He desires that the truth of His Word will go down deeply and transform us by His power and His Spirit. Sometimes, when the Lord moves in our lives, it takes time for us to get to a place of total surrender.

Sometimes, we resist the call to give up everything to follow Him. But when He calls us, it's just a matter of time. No matter the time it takes to get there, He is patient and merciful. He breathes life to those things that are dead through His redemptive power. It was at this season of my life as a teenage girl, I was about to move down a different road. It was a messed up road. A road of spiritual death and pain; a place I was never meant to travel but traveled because of my choice to disobey, and the heart of this little church-girl got broken.

Chapter 2

Help! What If I've Messed Up?

In 1985, two influential events happened in my life. The first was that our Bible Quiz team in Ypsilanti, Michigan, won the state, regional, and national championship. The other, though seemingly less historical, was that I began dating.

Since I was still very socially introverted and unconfident (especially around boys), this was an important event. It set the stage for the further cooling of my relationship with Christ and failure to guard my heart from the wrong affections. Honestly, Christ was probably never my first love at any stage yet in my life; He just dropped even farther down the list, and my new boyfriend took first place in my life. A boy from school that I had never noticed before (for good reason) began paying attention to me and I was very vulnerable. Every girl carries in her heart the desire to be loved and to feel lovely. The enemy will use whatever door he can enter to counterfeit a love that was designed to be received from only God, our Creator and Love.

Recipe for Disaster

Despite my parents' commitment to church, I was raised in an atmosphere, even at church, where the rite of passage for dating was simply turning sixteen. It had little to do with who you were dating, your emotional maturity, spiritual maturity, or the opinion of your parents. In hindsight, I do wish my parents would have put their foot down at the onset of this relationship. Though they disapproved of the young man and continued to disapprove for the next six years, they allowed me to date simply because I was sixteen and perhaps they thought they had no choice. With tight curfews and disapproving looks, I went off on my first date. I was naïve, vulnerable, desperately looking to be loved, and more than anything, I wanted to belong.

Of course, you know this is a recipe for disaster. How I wish someone would have had the courage to tell me this! Though a few brave youth workers tried, they never explained to me the "why" in keeping pure. It was always just the "what" and, unfortunately, that was no longer enough. It is one reason why I so passionately love to teach teenage girls the truth of who they are in Christ and why purity works for them, not against them.

Within weeks of dating, my heart was attached, and within months, my body followed. He was fun, the life of the party, and it helped me feel popular, something I had never felt before. Unfortunately, it was temporary and came at a great cost to my emotional well-being. You can imagine the problem when your identity, popularity, and longing for love comes at the hands of a pimple-faced, adolescent, non-Christian boy. *"Quite a setup for codependence and hurt"* is probably what comes into your mind. And it was. I am still kicking myself over it.

May I offer a word of wisdom to the parents of girls? *You have a wonderful opportunity and responsibility to lay a foundation of protection (emotionally and physically) from the schemes of the enemy for your daughter.*

Dad, you can date and show your daughter what it means to be loved and treated as lovely. You are the first man who will send her that message. If you don't, it will create a vacuum that leaves her vulnerable to someone who will. It also gives her a standard of what it looks like to be loved so that she can recognize what love doesn't look like. Start young and keep affirming her throughout her teen years, even when she pulls away from you. I know she may act as if she doesn't want you around. Don't worry—she is simply testing the waters and you. Part of her still desperately longs to remain your little girl; another part of her feels the surge of womanhood and independence. Regardless, her heart needs to feel loved and protected no matter what comes out of her mouth.

Mom, you have a responsibility to teach your daughter how to protect herself—physically, emotionally, and sexually. Though it may be a difficult hurdle for you, your silence is an enemy. Overcome it with godly truth. No matter the shame or lack of education in your past, she needs to know what to expect, what to do in a bad situation, and most importantly, she needs to know she can count on you no matter what foolish situation she has found herself in.

Though I look back with great remorse and regret over the foolish choices I made, I also see the hand and grace of God who protected me from even more dire consequences. Our daughters face even greater dangers in this present culture. There are too many predatory men in our culture who want to victimize and then discard our girls, as objects of self-gratification. I encourage you to be vigilant and unashamedly passionate about protecting your daughters!

When a girl is loved conditionally, it creates an insecure heart. She is never enough, so there is always a striving to maintain the acceptance of that conditional love. Insecurity fears rejection. It also fears being alone so much that it clings. When a girl strives to hold on securely, out of this insecure fear, she usually ends up driving love away.

This became the story of my life for the next six years. I threw myself into being the perfect girlfriend, compromising every ideal and moral I had believed in. My boyfriend was ill-equipped to meet my emotional needs and preferred to keep all of his options open, even while pretending to be in a committed relationship. Obviously, my insecurities increased as a result of his actions. Over and over, I let my heart be broken because I didn't see the value that I had as an image-bearer. I thought that if I changed enough, I could become someone he could really love. I played the church-girl on Sunday, but the rest of the week—like so many church kids—I lived a counterfeit Christianity. I even finished my last year of Bible Quiz still a champion (on the outside), but miserably sin-sick on the inside. Duplicity became a normal part of my life during those Bible Quiz matches as I mastered the art of quoting scriptures I had violated the night before. My parents' resistance to this relationship was too little, too late as they watched the impact it was having on my life.

When You Find Yourself Broken

So what was God thinking about me during all this? I had messed up. I wasn't even serving Jesus. If you would have told me that one day I would spend my life teaching the Word I was hypocritically quoting, I probably would have laughed. My heart, trying to compensate for my insecurities, became even more defiant and fractured as I sought to find my place in this new world apart from Christ. Though outwardly I appeared to be happy, I was miserable on the inside. The unfortunate downside for the prodigal who has memorized thirteen books of the New Testament is trying to live at peace with life apart from God. Stupid and quite impossible, at least for me.

The same enemy who lured me into this world enjoyed taunting me about my separation from God. I still believed that He existed. We just weren't talking any longer. As if He was an old friend I was angry with, I was holding a grudge. Yet, I still found myself terrified of the reality of eternity without Him. Perhaps some would suggest that this irrational fear was present because I'd been socially conditioned to the idea of God, and indoctrinated to fear hell and God's wrath through my fundamentalist upbringing. But life will make a liar out of any worldview that is inconsistent with reality. My reality was a real, intense, and dark torment that plagued me. I felt powerless against this fear of living life apart from God.

Whenever we subject ourselves to sin, we become slaves of that sin. Our own autonomy becomes a slave-master. It is the self-defeating deception of trying to live an autonomous life. Later, even as a Christ-follower and pastor's wife, I would have to work through this spirit of fear that engulfed me whenever I was alone in the dark. Our choices have consequences when we mess up.

Fortunately, choosing Christ opens the door to weapons that can defeat that darkness.

Despite my duplicity, I still maintained close connections to both my Bible Quiz coach and my Sunday school teacher. These two ladies were pivotal in my journey back to Christ and the church world. They prayed for me, talked to me, and invited me to continue playing softball on the women's church team. Unfortunately (or fortunately for me), this created an obligation to attend one service per week. My parents had moved out of town and I lived on my own, so I no longer had to go to church. It was now my choice. It was a sneaky trick they played, but I loved playing softball. I couldn't refuse, and kept going through the motions of church.

Since my parents had moved away, all of their opposition to my romantic relationship also seemed to move away with them. They still disapproved, but now their absence allowed me the freedom to come and go as I pleased without any nagging about what I was doing with my life. I find it profound that it was actually *this* change that opened my eyes to the dysfunction in my life and my relationship with my boyfriend. This young man had convinced me that I was better off living by his standards and definition of love. Suddenly, I realized that the problems in our relationship had nothing to do with my parents and their boundaries/restrictions, which had previously made him so unhappy. His love (or lack thereof) and treatment of me, along with my ugly compromises, were making me unhappy.

At the same time, I was being drawn back into the community of my church family. My two mentors convinced me to help coach the Junior Bible Quiz team of younger kids, which included one of their daughters. My agreement to help led to a designation of "head coach" that first night of JBQ. I am still not quite sure how that happened, but I see how their willingness to take a risk opened the door for God to work in my heart. Sometimes love must take a risk.

I loved those little kids. With all my heart, I saw children as a gift, and still do. I remember leaving JBQ practice feeling absolutely miserable about my life because suddenly I cared about someone else besides myself. What would they think of me if they saw me living this way? They were instrumental in softening my heart so God could speak redemption and healing to it.

A word of wisdom to the church at large: *we need to make a place in the body of Christ for the prodigal to return, just as they are.* So many times we want people who walk into our church to be sanctified because they might "influence" our children negatively. I believe that my children need opportunities—under my guidance— to interact with unbelieving people. If they never get that opportunity to sharpen their faith and stand for Christ while under our leadership, how will they handle it when they are out on their own? I'm not afraid of unbelievers, because I know the power of Christ transforms unregenerate hearts, especially when we live out our own transformation in front of them. I know this power because I've experienced it. Our children need to see this in action in the body of Christ. So my heart is forever grateful to those two beautiful ladies, Barb and Ellen, who took a risk and extended love and grace to me, even while I was a messed up sinner. It sounds an awful lot like Jesus and I think that is the point. The church was meant to look more like Jesus than themselves.

The end of my dark time in life, as I like to refer to it, culminated in the most unlikely place. It still makes me smile when I think of it. It was in the dance room of Lucille's, a little hole-in-the-wall bar, in Canton, Michigan. I'm not even sure if it is still standing today. Somehow, it was appointed by the Holy Spirit to be my meeting place with Jesus. Obviously, it is not a place I recommend for most people, but the grace of God found me there. It reminds me of that beautiful scripture in Psalm 139:7: "*Where can I go from your Spirit? Where can I flee from your presence?*" He found me there, in the most obscure place. Doesn't that sound like a beautiful rescue?

When God is working on a heart, it doesn't matter where we try to hide; He will flush us out. Indeed, He did flush me out of that place. My friend was on the dance floor having a great time, while I sat miserably drinking a cold beer (which I absolutely hated) and staring out at the scene.

Suddenly, it was a surreal moment as the Spirit of God spoke softly to my heart. *"Is this really what you want your life to be?"* His presence surrounded me and engulfed my heart so heavily that I ran out of the bar weeping. I couldn't stop. Years of hurt, shame, pain, and fear began to wash out of me. Soon, my friend joined me to find out what happened. She had been raised a church-girl, and she had enough discernment to know her night of partying was over.

As we drove home, I only remember telling her that God would not leave me alone and I couldn't do this any longer. She left me, confused and worn out at my apartment. That was Friday night. I don't remember the rest of the weekend. On Sunday, I walked into church and down the aisle to the altar. God had asked the question and I offered my answer. I don't recall if it was a salvation request. It didn't matter because I was determined to be at peace with God before He drove me crazy with His relentless love.

Rescued by Grace

Thus began my journey of healing and redemption. You probably have a story of a beautiful rescue, as well. Perhaps it was a story marred with shame, sin, and pain; but then it was perfectly covered and washed clean with the redemptive power of Christ. That's what makes it beautiful. It is so undeserved. His death gave Him all authority to cleanse everything away, leaving us very beautiful and spotless.

Sometimes we allow the past to disqualify us. *"I'm too messed up to be a pastor or pastor's wife!"* My friend, you were loved enough to be found by Him. Once you answer His invitation to come and receive His forgiveness, He covers you with the righteousness of Christ. You are no longer covered in filth, sin, or shame. I wonder how He feels when we continually point at our past as an excuse for not doing what He has asked. Each time He responds by pointing at the lovely righteousness of Jesus, for that is *all* He sees now. Does He ever want to shake us? Probably, just a bit.

If you are ever going to make peace with ministry, you must make peace with how you see yourself and your past. You must take off the old glasses and put on His glasses allowing Him to transform and renew your mind. His Word tells us we are a new creation. Redeemed. Washed. Sanctified. All of these wonderful words compel us to move on, beyond our past and into our present and future places of ministry. Don't you think it's time?

At my moment of decision, I had no idea what God was doing behind the scenes. He was working on so many different levels, preparing both my husband and I for a life of ministry. His grace kept that part hidden from me while He did a healing work on my heart and mind. I'm sure it would have terrified me.

Likewise, if you knew all that God had in mind for you, you would be overwhelmed. Yet you must make the choice to leave behind the old labels, ideas, and ways you've identified yourself so He can bring healing. You must be willing to let go of the past, if you want to experience all He has for you in the future. All I know today is this truth: *we find true freedom and peace when we respond in faith with our obedience to the drawing of His Spirit.* It will never work the other way around. I had a choice to make in that bar. If I resisted, I would have stayed stuck in the same place of hurt and brokenness. If you refuse to let go of shame and past sin, you will stay stuck. None of us can come to Christ for salvation on our own merit or righteousness. There are people in the church and outside the church who will try to convince you otherwise. All of us are guilty without Christ. I don't care how "churchy" you may have been before you found Christ. In fact, "churchy" is probably a hindrance to ministry, and God will have to purge all religiosity out of the religious person. It is only in your obedience through faith in Christ that you will find yourself on the journey to begin being the real (authentic, committed,) woman of God He created you to be. Only when your identity and life are hidden in Him will you truly be able to live at peace, no matter the scandal of the past.

Perhaps you have been a pastor's wife for many years but still find yourself always coming back to this place of shame or unworthiness. My friend, rather than give ear any longer to the intimidation of the enemy, it's time to give ear to this truth: *God loves being your Redeemer*. He finds great joy in taking your past mistakes—*which were meant to destroy you*—and use them to make a public spectacle of the enemy! Your pain can be turned into great passion. Your hurt can become a scar that reminds you to proclaim the healing power of Christ to others. Your brokenness can produce future generations of wholeness as a testimony of His grace.

What great joy it must bring Him to pull the rug on the enemy of our soul at the last moment with His redemptive power and bring greater fruitfulness in His eternal kingdom as a result of our redeemed lives! It is a brilliant, God-idea. No human could ever think it up and it's what I love most about my life in ministry—seeing other people's lives redeemed through His grace because I offered Him my "messed-up" life.

When you hear the accusations and condemning thoughts in your head, throw them back into the enemy's face, and move forward in obedient faith, trusting the call God has placed on your life and your future. Determine to let your life be a declaration of the unlimited patience of Jesus Christ. Seek to be empowered by the Spirit of God to do damage to the kingdom of darkness; for when you do, you become dangerous. A free woman is a dangerous woman. It is the cry of my heart as a pastor's wife to leave a lasting kingdom impact on the world God has placed me in, and I pray it will become yours as well. I think it might make God smile just a bit, when He sees it. And I don't know about you, but more than anything else, I want to make Him smile.

Chapter 3

Help! I Don't Like Change!

There is no denying the reality that the move into full-time, or even part-time, ministry brings about great change. If you are like most people, change comes with great difficulty. But it can also come with great benefits. I find it interesting that God created a universe filled with constant change. Time rolls on, whether we like it or not. The universe holds all the dynamics of birth, growth, and yes, even aging. In spite of all of this, one of the most beautiful characteristics of God is His unchanging nature.

Does it seem strange that in the midst of all of this change, He remains the same? You know the saying, "Yesterday, today, and forever, the same." How—or the better question—why, is this the case? Perhaps the best way for us to deal with the change that life (and ministry) thrusts upon us is to place our confidence and hope in something that is not changing. Perhaps just as He holds the universe together, He can hold us together.

While my rededication to Christ had indeed been a powerful experience, the sanctification process that began that day was definitely more challenging. When Christ frees a heart from sin, it is a profound miracle. What is also profound is the power that the believer now has through the Holy Spirit to walk in the authority and freedom of Christ. What we were once powerless against, we now have authority, through Jesus Christ, to overcome. Yet, I mentioned an important truth in the last chapter: we must *choose* to align ourselves in obedience to God, and then the Holy Spirit empowers us to walk in freedom. God is not a puppet master who takes control of us and, against our will, demands obedience. That would never bring us into a greater intimacy and dependency on Christ.

Embracing Change

The first step in embracing change gracefully is to *agree with God* about where He is taking you. Is your heart filled with resentment or resistance over the changes demanded of you because you are a pastor's wife? I confess that some days I do struggle with the changes that following Christ into ministry has brought into my life. Most of them caused extreme discomfort, something I don't like. Few of us do.

You've probably discovered, along with me, that sometimes life throws us a curve-ball—on second thought, *many* times life throws us a curve ball. At those times, it is important to rise up and do our best to connect with the ball even if we don't like or aren't comfortable with change. If you refuse to get in the batter's box, or half-heartedly take swings at the pitches coming your way, you will be miserable. So will your spouse. The root of most of our resentment or resistance is that we feel that God is being unfair when He asks us to change. We don't agree that the change is good for us, so we put up resistance. Or for many of us, it can be that ministry is harder than we realized; it is certainly less glamorous. This couldn't be what He had in mind! And for some, it may be that letting go of our expectations and personal desires is harder than we realized.

My own journey to healing and preparation for ministry began with small, obedient steps, a great deal of discomfort, and many stumbles along the way. My heart for six years had been emotionally and socially attached to my ex-boyfriend, and my fear of being alone had kept me committed to that relationship. Letting go of all of this was terribly frightening. I had a choice to make. However, I didn't really have to ask God what He thought about this relationship. I already knew. Though desperately painful and uncomfortable, I made the choice to walk away. I discovered that when I chose to walk in obedience, God poured out His grace to help me walk it out. It was difficult, but doable.

This is the power of the Spirit in the life of a believer. We must come into agreement with whatever God is asking. It may be difficult, it may not look as glamorous as you imagined, it may mean letting go of where you thought your life should be or what it would look like, but when you agree with God through your obedience, you find peace and joy one obedient step at a time.

The next step in embracing change is recognizing that God did not call you into the ministry to punish you. Having been in ministry for over twenty years, I realize some people that come your way can feel like a punishment! However, this is not the truth. Jesus tells us in John 5:17 that God is always working, and Paul reminds us that He is working for our *good.* (Romans 8:28) This winning combination is pivotal to your freedom in enjoying ministry life.

Despite what you feel, He hasn't forgotten you and it is certainly not His intention to harm you. He is working all things together for the good, so trust that He is growing you into the woman He knows you can be. You have chosen to align yourself with God. You have stepped into an agreement with Him to bring His kingdom to earth by your service. If this is the case, you are in the best position you can be in. It is a position of allowing God to work for your good. He is not harming you by your place of ministry, not even when those difficult people come your way. He is working to make your life look less like you, and more like Him. This is a long, and sometimes, arduous process, especially, if your life looked anything like mine. You must come to peace with Him in this area, my friend. He is not trying to make you fail. If you don't accept this, you can easily fall into the snare of bitterness or cynicism that too many pastors or pastor's wives have been trapped by. Too many walk around as if pastoring is a burden that must be endured, rather than a privilege to be enjoyed.

It helps to remind ourselves that God is *always* good. We must not only think it, believe it, and meditate upon it, but we must step out in faith to the testimony of that truth. Our actions will reflect what we really believe about God. If we believe that He is not for us, we will resent or resist Him. If, on the other hand, we trust that

He is for us and operating out of a heart of love for our best, we can safely take that risky step into change.

A few years ago, I had the privilege of sharing my story to a group of women while teaching a class on emotional healing from sexual sin. This is a tender topic. So many women have been hurt and are now overwhelmed with condemnation or shame over their past (or current) sexual sin. Having been there, I quietly prayed and asked the Holy Spirit to help me speak truth and freedom.

After I shared my story (and it is still very hard to do) and the truth of God's Word on the subject, the discussion opened up for questions from the ladies. There were tears and confessions. But there was one thing that surprised me. It seemed that in the minds of some of these precious women, God could not be trusted. I sensed the impact their hurt from men had had on their ability to trust anyone, even God. As we talked about walking away from our sexual sin, even if it required walking away from an immoral relationship, I also sensed some dangerous rationalization taking place. It was a rationalization that says this: *"Maybe God freed you and gave you grace to walk away and find healing, but it's different for me."*

I must confess that I felt a bit of irritation rise up inside me at the danger of this lie. While I admit it *had* been a difficult and painful process, it was certainly possible. Why couldn't they see the possibilities of change that Christ could bring into their lives? It had only been done through the power of Christ at work in my life. It had nothing to do with me, and everything to do with Him. Maybe they thought it was easier for me, because I was the pastor's wife. There will be some in the church who believe that you have an easier path of grace because you are a pastor's wife. I encourage you to resist this thought process. This is a deception from the enemy to keep people from gaining freedom over sin. And it really makes me sad. When they agree with this lie, they lose hope of ever being free. While God is no respecter of persons, He *is* a respecter of obedient faith. (Heb. 11:6) If we choose to yield ourselves into God's hands, we will find all the grace and power (though we may feel weak) to walk in freedom from sin and ungodly relationships. He is not setting us up to watch us fall on our face so He can ridicule us. Every person who comes to Christ must choose to walk away from their sin or not. There is no shortcut for people in ministry—not even the pastor's wife. God doesn't play favorites in the faith department and He doesn't find pleasure in punishing us.

The road to graceful change is marked with potholes, ditches, and many landmines. Each step requires aligning yourself with God, believing that He is good, and yielding to God those things, ideas, and attitudes that oppose Him. I recall times of extreme loneliness during the first year after surrendering my life wholly to Christ. I found my heart yearning for connection with my old friends, even my old boyfriend, at times. Though I went back a few times and tried to toy with those old relationships, in my heart I felt God continue to insist that I release them. They weren't good for me and would only sidetrack me from what He had in mind.

What about you? Do you have expectations, attitudes, or dreams that you need to release to God? Maybe it's an expectation you've never even mentioned to your spouse, but deep down you struggle to fully embrace the change ministry brings because you are holding on to it. Maybe you struggle with your affections. Are they wrapped around material wants or needs? Do you see ministry as a hindrance to those things you wanted in life? This can be hard for all of us, especially when our culture is so materially-minded and labels success according to what we possess. Most people (outside of ministry) don't understand the cost of ministry. It's not just the financial cost; it's the loss of time, privacy, and free space in your brain. I, too, still battle the sacrifices and costs (emotionally, physically, and financially) of ministry from time to time in this area. It has been very important during those struggles to not allow my mind to wander into the "what-if" of a life outside of ministry. Jesus told us not to build a life of storing up material things, but to seek first His kingdom and all of the things that we have need of will be given to us.

God knows all of our dreams, but if He has called us to ministry, it's time to release those dreams and let Him give them back to you repackaged and reenergized by His Spirit. Give Him those things He is asking from you and trust that He will give back to you in greater portion than you could ever possibly give.

A Return Investment

Coming to Christ cost me a great deal. I let go of not just a long-term relationship, but also most of my friends. When you give up friends and a partying life, your schedule comes to a screeching halt. My memories of believing I was the *only* girl home alone on Friday and Saturday nights while I wept and cried out to God come flooding back to me even today. It was an intense emotional battle and there was a great deal of warfare. I had strongholds that had to be broken, removed, and healed up.

At that time, I never imagined what He had in mind. I couldn't see a husband, a family, or an opportunity to serve in His Kingdom in such a beautiful way. I only saw my empty, quiet apartment. I had to choose in faith to allow Him to change things as He saw fit and step into that change willingly, embracing it and Him. It all came down to one thing each time I found myself struggling: *Did I trust God enough with my future to give Him the gift of my obedience in the present?* My past had left me hollow and empty, so as I wept before the Lord on those evenings, I came to know and trust His unchanging nature and love for me. It was truly one of the most profound growing times in my life. I was learning to really *know* God and choosing daily to make Him my first love. So I made my choice—over and over again—every time those feelings would come. These are some of the great opportunities that change can bring. By embracing the change, we force ourselves to grow in intimacy with Christ. Whether we are in ministry or not, we are called to love God above everything else. We can offer it up, or we can go down kicking and screaming. The speed at which we get there depends upon our willingness to bend to the change He is asking.

Sometimes when we are called into ministry life, we are afraid. Afraid of what other people will think about us. Afraid of the price ministry may cost our family or friends. Perhaps you've settled into the reality that God has asked you to do this and He is good, but what about the church? We all know that, sometimes, *they* aren't good. Some of them can be downright cruel. It is one thing to take a risk personally, but it's another thing to put your children or family at risk. These are all legitimate fears that you must face. While it would be crazy to tell you that it won't happen (as it does sometimes), I can tell you that the same God who is working in you is also working in the lives of your friends and family. He doesn't operate on you in a vacuum! He is thinking much farther down the generational line than either of one of us can think.

When you choose to go into ministry, people will question your qualifications. They may question your mental state. You will get strange looks and, sometimes, very silent responses, especially from people who don't follow Christ. This is normal—not too pleasant—but entirely normal. They may ask you all the questions that have been fearfully running through your own head. Guard your mind from giving fear a place in your mind. You must rest in the reality that God hasn't given you the luxury of all the answers ahead of time. Your life in ministry will, and should, surprise you. I think you will find eventually that this is part of the joy of ministry. In fact, I find God has an incredibly perfect sense of timing, and an even greater sense of humor. The question will be: *are we preparing and readying ourselves in obedience to that timing?*

In the midst of my brand new decision to walk with Christ, I encountered another curve ball. It was the new youth pastor. Suddenly I was faced with the reality of a life in ministry. I was in no position to ever believe that I was called to ministry. I was just trying to keep my head above water, while turning my life raft around to go in the right direction.

My problem was that I found myself liking Carey—*really* liking him. I forced it out of my head. I had also committed to refrain from dating for a long while so the Lord could bring healing to my insecure and damaged heart. This complicated things a bit, but what resulted was even better. It was the beginning of great friendship. This friendship became the foundation for a healthy marriage, and to this day, it is still one of my favorite things about being married to my husband. He truly is my best friend, and I find the joy of sharing my life, laughter, and crazy dreams with him second to none. So we became friends first. He watched a young girl struggle and stumble to allow God to put the pieces of her heart back together. I watched God take an inexperienced, but willing, humble youth pastor and grow him into a man of character and great vision so one day he would be capable of leading a home and a great church.

It was important to both of us (though we never verbalized it until much later) that we both be committed to Christ first. I had mixed that up before. It was important to me that I serve Christ because I loved Him and trusted Him, not to find a husband. My advice to single ladies out there: *set your heart into the hands of God, and refuse to take it back.* He can be trusted to keep it safe. When the time is right, He will release you to share it with the man He desires to have it. Until that day, cultivate your love life with Jesus. Set your affections on eternity and your life with Christ. It will mean saying "no" to the good, in exchange for God's best. I say this with all the gentleness I can, for I truly do understand the desire of a heart to be married and loved by a husband. I remember painfully what loneliness looked like. But I also remember what I discovered when I faced that intimidating loneliness with Jesus at my side: *I was never really alone.* Sometimes the fear of something is greater than the thing itself. My surrender to Christ had ensured His constant presence and protective covering every day. The enemy of loneliness, once faced, was now not so strong. Turn and face it, rather than continually running from it. If you do, you, too, will discover that truth.

Moving Out of The Past

My life radically changed over the course of just a couple years. As a structured and very schedule-oriented woman, I really can say I don't like change. Not many of us do. But some things in our lives must change if we are going to be ready for God to use us. Isn't that what following Christ is really all about? Following implies moving. Jesus didn't say, *"Stand here with me."* He said, *"Follow me."* Are we willing to pick up our crosses and follow Him regardless of what we must leave behind?

Some things need to be left behind. Obviously, our sin and shame, but what about our comforts and expectations? There are seasons where our lives must be radically churned up, so that real growth and ministry can take place. It is never easy to let go of the past, but it is necessary. It may be necessary to release the pictures of the ideal life you have held on to. You cannot imagine what God has ahead for you. His ways and His story are so much greater than any ideal story you or I can conjure up. Letting go may include past labels or identities that others have placed on you. Free yourself from those, too. They no longer define you. No matter what was spoken over you before this day, you are new creation in Christ, and it is His value that now gives you worth. Refuse to place your value anywhere else.

After many months of talking and building the foundation of friendship with my husband; it became evident that our feelings for each other were growing. While I honestly never saw myself in ministry or desired the position of *pastor's wife*, I truly can say that I had no doubt about marrying my husband. He may have had some doubts about marrying me with all my baggage! For the first time in a relationship, I felt my heart was protected both by God, and by Carey.

About a year and half after meeting each other, my husband rented a plane (he is a pilot), flew us to Indianapolis, and proposed to me. He is a romantic at heart. That night, we ate dinner in a wonderful restaurant overlooking the Hoosier Dome and ended the evening with a beautiful winter carriage ride. It was all quite a whirlwind for both of us. Our engagement and wedding played out in the spotlight of ministry at my home church. Nine months later, we were married, and I was now a pastor's wife. The excitement ended quickly as we began our new journey together.

Within a couple months of marriage, we accepted a call to start a youth ministry in a very young home mission's church in northern Michigan. We left our friends, our church, our jobs, and our city. It was a blur and a radical lifestyle change. We arrived in Traverse City in November, and I cried for the entire winter. It was the longest winter of my life. Well, almost. Living in Traverse City, we have a tendency to say that *every* year.

I found myself suddenly overwhelmed as I tried to navigate my new life being married to a pastor. All of us will have seasons of great change in ministry. At times, the change that ministry brings your life will be overwhelming. Other times, you may feel emotionally drained from it all. But trust that God will sustain you and breathe new life into your troubled heart and mind as you navigate the winter of change.

One day, you will feel warmth again as you reach a place of new life. You will begin to see pockets of hope and beauty in the place He has planted you. Until then, know He is willing to hold everything together for you, and give you what you need, until you are stronger. Lean into His strong, unchanging arms during the change process. You may not understand it. You still may not like it. But choose to make yourself clay in His hands. Your mind cannot imagine the beautiful vessel He is creating out of you.

Chapter 4

Help! I Can't See Where I'm Going!

"Can a blind man lead a blind man? Will they not both fall into a pit? A student is not above his teacher, but everyone who is fully trained will be like his teacher." (Luke 6:39-40)

When Jesus shared this parable, he was speaking to the religious leaders of his day who were hypocritically pointing out every flaw they detected in the lives of their congregants, while overlooking their own decayed and wretched state. He was asking them, *"Aren't you both just destined to fall into the pit unless you, the religious leaders, get your act together?"* Truer words were never spoken.

As ministry leaders, we have an incredible responsibility to lead people down the path of truth, not only with our words, but with the example of our lives. Our top priority must be to live a life wholly submitted to the Lordship of Christ as we lead; otherwise, we are just dropping people into a ditch and leaving them there. If we can't live in freedom and led by the Spirit, how can they? Words are easy; living it out is much harder. So if we are leaders, where are we leading?

The moment you step into ministry, you set your foot in opposition to an intimidating foe. He will seek to discourage, disillusion, and, eventually, destroy you and the part you play in God's story. While this is true for all believers in Christ, I know that the place of a pastor involves an even greater amount of opposition because of the potential influence to good—or do harm—to the body of Christ.

The primary purpose of this book is to reach out and grab the hand of the pastor's wife and tell her, "*You can do this! You are exactly who God has in mind for the job of leading this church!"* Whether you have come into your position through marriage to a pastor, or a vocational change as a couple, it is not mistake. I know it can feel like a mistake, but God knows exactly what your church needs and He chose you and your husband to lead them. Together, you are all on a path to become more like Jesus Christ, and grow your leadership skills in the process! So what better place to make that happen than in your current place of ministry? By the way, I highly recommend that if you are going to thrive in ministry, you learn to tap into your sense of humor—whatever little bit you may have—and grow it a lot! The less intense you are about yourself and your position, the better off you will be.

Free to Be Me

As a new pastor's wife, I was clueless about my position and I really think that was God's grace. Too much information on what to expect would have sent my Type-A tendencies into overdrive and driven everyone else crazy.

Sometimes we have misconstrued ideas about how we must behave spiritually when we become the pastor's wife. This is especially true when you have transitioned from layperson to ministry. I think that transitioning from layperson to pastor, in your home church, is one of the most difficult transitions because people already know you. Overnight you go from just a normal person (*whatever that means*) to a new title of "pastor" or "pastor's wife". They may know a lot about you, including the mistakes of your past. And your past may include some of them. In fact, there may be parts of you that they don't necessarily like.

Some may resent your transition, or are troubled by the realization they are suddenly forced to face: *a pastor is really just a regular person.* We want to put people on pedestals. We want to believe that there are different levels of people, especially spiritually, with some more deserving, and some undeserving. We like to follow people we can look up to. It becomes easy to put on a mask when we step into leadership and try to be someone we were never meant to be. The pressure is on us to have all the answers, to be the perfect wife and mother, and to make everyone in the church happy. Run from this pressure.

Remember this truth: **God alone has all the answers.** You and your husband are imperfect; you will never please everyone in your church; and yes, you *will* even yell at your children from time to time! All of us do. When you become a ministry leader, you aren't transformed into someone else miraculously overnight. You are still dealing with the same set of strengths and weaknesses you had before you were in ministry. You are in the same marriage with the same character issues. You still have the same knowledge base (though it will help to be committed to growing it as a leader) as you did the day before you went into ministry. You get the idea. There, hopefully, *will* be an awesome transformation
over time as the Lord is free to deal with you. If you recognize your need for His help and are committed to being yourself, it goes a long way in being the leader He wants you to be. God has dealt a long time with my perfectionism and need to please people, so I want to encourage you to live free from the start. I am grateful that He is so patient because that toxic duo of people-pleasing and needing to have all the answers was a difficult challenge to overcome.

A few years after we became lead pastors, I decided to go back to college to finish my degree. I felt a draw to social work and started school with a husband, two kids, and a church. I remember taking my first counseling course and feeling very excited because I had been in ministry for quite a few years. I had already counseled many people so this class was going to be breeze! I can't recall if I volunteered to do that first session role-playing, or not. I probably did, and all that overconfidence should have been a red flag. To this day I don't even recall the other person's make-believe problem, but as soon as the scenario was given, I jumped in with both feet and my pastor's wife expertise.

I went through the role-playing with flying colors; everything was neat and quickly tied up in about ten minutes. I turned and looked at my instructor feeling very good about the session. He had the strangest look on his face. He looked at me and said, *"You have just managed to break just about all the rules of counseling and attempt to "fix" this girl in record time, less than ten minutes!"*

He was obviously not impressed and I was confused. What was his problem? Wasn't the goal to fix her problem? He explained quickly to the class (and me) that counseling is not about "fixing" people. Having all the answers was not the primary goal. It was also about building relationships, displaying empathy and understanding, and empowering people to change on their own. It was a humbling, and yet very important lesson for me.

As pastors, one of our primary roles is to *equip* the church to do the work of the ministry. Not *fix* the church. I still battle the tendencies to "fix" people with all the right answers, right books, and some easy 3-step solutions. But as leaders, we aren't called to do that. We are to live life with them, build relationships, equip them to follow Christ, and most importantly, lead them by example. We are called to lead them to Jesus where He can be free to work in their lives. We don't need to know everything, and we, certainly, aren't supposed to be perfect.

God, in His omniscience, has nothing hidden from Him so all of our pride, pretense, and artificiality will fall apart in His presence anyway. Yet He still chose us, so He must believe that we are capable of leading best when we are free to be ourselves. He deals with us on the line of who we *are* right now, not who we pretend or desire to be. The sooner we recognize this, the sooner He is free to mold us into the leaders that bring Him the most glory. Then we can find great fulfillment and freedom in leading. He isn't asking us to be perfect, or have all the answers for our congregation. He is looking for servants who are willing to learn and grow into leaders who have a heart and love for His church and kingdom.

Knocking the Chip off Your Shoulder

Just as we need to guard against the idea of perfectionism, there is also another opposite idea; an idea that is equally off-base and dangerous.

Sometimes, as a defense against the need to be perfect, the pastor's wife can put on her rebel t-shirt and take a more defensive approach. It may sound a lot like this, "*Like it or not, I don't care what you think about me. I am who I am!*" This is not love and it is *not* good leadership. It reeks of pride, insecurity, and fear; because it is really a smokescreen for all three and it will render us ineffective and hardened in ministry.

I have encountered individuals in ministry who were so defensive that it was frustrating, and virtually impossible, to work with them. You just couldn't teach them anything because they already knew everything. Being around people like that is very much like walking on eggshells. Every correction is a threat. Every attempt to help them grow in leadership results in a thicker wall of defensiveness. But that defensiveness is really just a self-preservation mechanism against the fear of being vulnerable and seen as imperfect. And the cost of a defensive heart is great. You incur the loss of meaningful and healthy relationships. You lose great wisdom and guidance for ministry and life when you put up a defensive wall from people who are meant to help you. You lose the opportunity to truly receive and give love to others.

Eventually, you'll weary those around you with your resistance and walls. People will only walk on eggshells for so long, before they will give up and move on. To live without the willingness to risk love and intimacy is to really never live at all. It is like being the walking dead. My friend, if you find yourself here, will you consider these words from a *safe and impartial* sister in ministry? God is the only defense you need. You cannot defend yourself perfectly from pain or rejection. Your husband cannot always keep you safe. He shouldn't be put in such an awful position, either. To pit your husband against his church is an unloving thing to do. Tear down the walls you've thrown up around yourself and allow

God to free you to really love the people you serve. There is great value in the friendships you can have within your church family. There is so much value in the sharpening that takes place when we make ourselves real and vulnerable to others. To refuse keeps us shriveled up emotionally and stuck in our insecurities.

God is the only One who can keep your heart whole so that it is free to give and receive love, even in the face of rejection. We are *all* works in progress, as leaders and followers of Christ! God is not content to leave you like you are, because just like me, you are in need of sanctification. If you stifle that, you risk stifling the Spirit of God in your heart and you become ugly and bitter against ministry and His people. This is a miserable combination; no good for your church or your marriage.

The Ostrich Approach

Finally, the last leadership approach I want to address is the ostrich approach. Now truthfully, the ostrich gets a bad rap. The ostrich is notorious for burying its head in the sand to avoid trouble. But I discovered this year, while teaching science to my nine-year-old, that the ostrich is not burying its head out of cowardice. In fact, the ostrich mother, when danger approaches, refuses to leave the nest of her babies and instead stretches out her neck and flattens herself so her enemy does not see her or her babies. When the babies are born, they are in danger from hawks. They learn from their mother to stretch out and flatten when danger approaches to avoid being eaten. (I just felt the need to defend the ostrich, in spite of the analogy I am about to use.)

Sometimes the pastor's wife takes the approach that ministry is her husband's "job" and doesn't need to be her "job" too. She buries her head in the sand and refuses to engage in any part of ministry. There are a variety of reasons this will happen. Some are pure motives, others not so pure. Maybe it's ignorance. If that is the case, ministry is about to give her an education. Churches don't just hire pastors, they hire pastoral families. (I will discuss this in-depth in my chapter on PK's and marriage.) You may see it as his job, but your church rarely will. This can cause you all a great deal of tension.

What I am about to say is my personal opinion and not a theological stance. It comes from over twenty years of experience of discovering what works best. Choosing to be a pastor is answering a "call" to serve Jesus. It is not serving a paycheck, or even just serving a church. If we served for just a paycheck, it would be a great disappointment in most cases. While we are serving the church for Jesus, ultimately, we are not doing it to please the church, but to lead the church. This makes ministry different than a typical vocation. As a pastor, your spouse is saying, *"Let me show you how to follow Christ in every area of your life by my words, leadership, and example."* He really needs you to help him in this.

My husband cannot show a woman how to be a godly wife, mother, or a godly woman. He can tell her, but if there is no one there to show her, a piece is missing. I recognize that there are single pastors who do a great job without a spouse. Usually, though, they are wise enough to tap into a godly female leader to help them fill this gap within the church. This, too, can work well. But your marriage also represents a partnership of vision to lead your family. If God has given your family a vision of leading a church, what will your non-participation speak? I fear it conveys a message that too many women already hear: *unity in the family vision is optional.*

If you are not in unity to the call to ministry, this is worked out best before you step into ministry. If you are already in ministry, I encourage you both to work this out quickly and come to a unified agreement so it won't affect your leadership ability.

If your motive for refusing to take part in leading the church is one of intimidation or fear, I encourage you to take this fear to Jesus and begin to let Him work this out of your heart. You have a great deal to offer your church. You may not be a natural-born leader, but some of the best pastor's wives aren't. You don't have to be on the stage to be a leader. Be a leader who is committed to showing others how to follow Jesus every day in the small things. Be a leader who can display what it looks like to gracefully love her husband. Be a leader who can show other women what it looks like to trust Jesus during the difficult seasons of life. Be a leader who can find the joy in life. You love Jesus, or I doubt that you would even step into ministry. Trust that God has a reason for putting you in this place of leadership. He believes you can serve your church well with your life.

Maybe you fear the "stereotypical" roles that pastors' wives have played in the past. Let go of those fears. The church, at large, has moved out of those stereotypes, and if your church hasn't, maybe you are put there to gracefully lead them away from those old constricting ideas.

I have watched many men struggle with the "absent" wife. When I use the word "absent", I am not referring to a woman who works outside the home. I, too, worked a full-time (and later, part-time) job outside the home for many years. You can still be in ministry while working outside the home. "Absent" implies a woman who wants no part of being a part of the church body, or helping her husband in their ministry call. It can be physically absent, but it is also emotionally or spiritually absent. One husband I knew struggled so much with his wife's detached approach, he finally gave up. For him, it was not any fun to serve alone. It was too compartmentalized, and he was always in tension between these two loves. She was fortunate. Sometimes a husband will fill the desired companionship in an unhealthy or immoral way. This is very wrong. I am not saying that this absence is the *cause* of his immorality. A husband has a responsibility to God, and to his wife, to resist this type of sin, but I do see how easily the enemy can set up traps for ministry couples. Keep in mind that it also works both ways. Her emotional absence to him can open the door for someone else to emotionally fill her vacuum.

Guard yourself from the ostrich trap. Your husband will need you throughout the ministry journey. Whether it is a discerning word, a comforting hand, or simply just your committed belief in the vision God has given him, he needs you. You will need each other. Lift your head up out of the intimidation and realize you can love and find joy in being the pastor's wife. Together you can serve better and grow stronger in your marriage as a result. (I will elaborate more on this later.)

Becoming a Servant Leader

My husband likes to say this to our church: *"To go up in the kingdom, you must be willing to give up."* I think this is one of the truest statements I have ever heard about leadership. You can take two approaches to this statement. You can embrace it or resent it.

Leadership has a cost. You have a responsibility to God for the people you lead. Even the pastor's wife must see this to avoid causing pain or being a stumbling block to her church. James 3:1 says this: *"Not many of you should presume to be teachers, my brothers, because you know that we who teach will be judged more strictly."*

Leadership does not merely give us influence and privileges, it gives us responsibility. What we do with that responsibility is important. When we ask people to follow us, we need to accept the responsibility to now live a crucified life. It is a cost of our time, our emotions, our finances, and so much more. Are you willing to give up, to go up and serve more people? Sometimes we get that mixed up and believe the church is there is to serve us. This is a mistake.

Paul teaches this philosophy so well. 1 Corinthians 9 is a rant about the rights of an apostle (Paul) and then he follows up with this beautiful declaration of servant leadership. 9:12b *"But we did not use this right. On the contrary, we put up with anything rather than hinder the gospel of Christ."* Oh, that our leaders today would grab hold of this truth! There is little that God won't do when a leader takes this attitude. When we embrace our leadership as the work of the gospel, we become free to let God work in, and through us, in great ways. Listen to Paul go on (v.19), *"Though I am free and belong to no man, I make myself a slave to everyone, to win as many as possible."*

Servant leadership is about the freedom to serve the gospel. Giving up my rights, time, or money becomes a gift that I give to serve the gospel. I don't want to resent the gospel, but serve it and see my gift as sacrifice of worship. It really is about your attitude.

Let me address a new leadership challenge. Social media has radically changed our lives. I believe it has changed ministry as well. The ability to have a platform for the gospel through social media is astounding. But there are dangers. It also provides a platform for opinions, relationship drama, and offenses.

Paul says in 1 Corinthians 10:23-24: *"Everything is permissible"—but not everything is beneficial. "Everything is permissible"—but not everything is constructive. Nobody should seek his own good, but the good of others.* As leaders, my husband and I have taken this approach to our use of social media. We are here to serve the gospel and play a part in God's story. Before we write, post, or rant about anything on Facebook, Google+, Twitter, or anywhere else, we ask ourselves this question: *"Is this beneficial for the gospel?"* If not, we choose to steer clear. A servant leader sees the gospel as his or her first loyalty.

Our other ideas, political views, preferences, and personal rights must take a back seat to that. If my rant will cause people to stumble, I will not rant. If commenting on someone's drama will divide the body, I will not comment. I may be right. You may be right. But our greatest service is to the gospel. On the flip side, there are times when the leader must speak up to defend the gospel. I prefer to speak up in a venue where I can explain things clearly. It is tough to do this on Facebook or Twitter.

During a particular difficult season, I remember battling my willingness to give up my rights. With social media, people can slander and hurt with even greater vigilance. We had a woman who had left the church and was particularly nasty on social media. She never missed an opportunity to shoot spears at our church, our staff, and our leadership. I am a bit of hot-head, sometimes—okay, most of the time. Maybe it's the red hair, but more likely it was my flesh wanting to defend itself and prove she was wrong! It was hard to sit and take that type of social media abuse.

But the Lord gave me great strength and old-fashioned Holy Spirit direction when I would start to type out a rant: *"Don't do it."* This was always His answer. He would never release me to say anything. Coincidently, my husband gave me the same instructions. It was very frustrating because she was wrong. Didn't both of them know that? Out of that frustration came one of my greatest spiritual lessons in leadership. God began to show me that as a leader, it is not about being right, but it's always about *doing* what is right. We are examples to our church and they are watching. We are showing them how to "*do right*" in these frustrating situations, especially on social media.

In his book, My Utmost for His Highest, Oswald Chambers said, *"The fact that we insist on proving we are right is almost always a clear indication that we have some point of disobedience."* Sometimes my desire to rant was because I still had some pride buried deep down. Sometimes I just wanted to sling mud back at her. We have to be honest and let God work in us through these situations. If we begin to hurl spears at people in disobedience, there can be unintended consequences because others are watching. It can sow division and discouragement in those who are watching. Maybe you feel better after you say it, but does someone else? Is the gospel served by our right to be heard? There is a time and a place, but it is usually not in the context of social media snippets.

It is very important that we realize that God does not sit around in heaven choosing sides. We are the ones who must pick the correct side—or not. Will we choose to be on His side? He is on the side of truth. He is on the side of *what* is right, not *who* is right. If we understand this, we will carefully choose to give up our rights when it matters to best serve the gospel.

Lead With What Is In Your Hand

One of the greatest gifts my husband gave to me (and he has given me many) was the freedom to be myself. His approach has been always to allow me the freedom to serve where I felt God's pleasure. Finding the place where your talents and passions intersect with God's partnership is profoundly fulfilling.

I love horses. I have loved them since I was a small child. However, I was not able to actually get my first horse until I was forty-one years old. It was a long waiting process, for sure. I also love speaking to girls about everything girl-related. After I got my first horse, I prayed, *"God, all that I have belongs to You; use it in any way You desire"* I spent this past summer kicking off our *LifeWorks Girls* program working on a ranch with—guess what? Yes, horses. There are few words to describe the feeling it is to work where you feel God's pleasure best. How do you know where this is? Answer these questions:

- *Where do you feel most alive?*
- *What can you do that requires hard work but you experience great joy?*
- *What are those things that leave you with a sense that you can do it forever and still enjoy it?*
- *Where do your passions come alive?*

Too many people inside and outside of ministry never take the time to answer these questions; they never try new things; or they are miserable because they put themselves into a ministry "box," never realizing that God can use whatever He puts in our hand and our heart for His glory and we can find true pleasure in serving. You aren't restricted to playing the piano, leading the women's ministry, or organizing every church dinner. (If you feel God's pleasure in these things, do them!) I used to be intimidated by so many things I felt I *couldn't* do, that I missed out on the joy of the things I *was* doing.

As you journey through ministry and life, your passions and interests may change. Occasionally, you will find (especially in a smaller pastorate) that you must do things that you don't really like to do. This is true in every vocation in life. My family is wonderful and I love them, but if I am truly honest I can't stand doing laundry. It is the most tedious and redundant task on the planet. I confess that I despise all things tedious and redundant. And please don't make me repeat that! Doing something over is such a chore to my task-oriented brain. But because I love my family, I understand that it comes with the package.

Sometimes in ministry, we can become stiff-necked and obstinate about what we don't want to do. Are we servants or prima-donnas? I know God has called me to love in this order: *God, my husband, my children, my extended family, my church.* Sometimes I can best love God by doing the tedious task. Sometimes I can best love my husband and relieve his pressure by stepping in and helping out for a time in a place that is less than thrilling to me. When my children were in the nursery, I served faithfully. This was my responsibility as a parent. I know that God has given me the responsibility to steward my children and to know what is going on in their lives whether in the nursery, children's ministry, or youth ministry. This is my calling as a *mother.* Don't despise the small jobs that are outside of your passions. Realize that things are for a season, not forever.

When we find ourselves in a position or place of leadership, always see it from the perspective of a servant. God teaches us so many wonderful things through those moments of servant-hood. The sooner we drop our expectations of who we need to be, or should be, the sooner we can become the leader God desires us to be. Give Him the freedom to use you anyway He desires. He will also surprise you with the things that are in your hands that He can use.

Ask yourself: *How can I serve these people best? How can I walk, not in perfection, but in love and humility before them as I follow Christ?* When we take on the posture of a servant, it forces our eyes off of ourselves, off of our congregation, and unto God. This is where our eyes need to stay for the remainder of our ministry journey.

Chapter 5

Help! I Can't Find the Fences!

For the sheer purpose of survival, the topic of boundaries must be broached quickly in the life of every pastor and pastor's wife. Most everyone agrees, after their first year in ministry, that ministers face an overwhelming sense of responsibility. This can become taxing in a situation where there are *good* boundaries in place. With weak or poor boundaries, it can become disastrous.

Boundaries are fences we place in our lives not only to give us limits, but also to give others limits that protect us. Contrary to what your congregation may think, or even what you may think, you are limited in the number of people you can serve at one time. That's why I believe it is so very important to invest early in building a strong team around you that can help you carry the load of ministry. This team may be staff, or it may be mature volunteer leaders in your church. It is better to build this team first. If you don't, you will find yourself perpetually frustrated, angry, or just plain worn out. When you first begin your ministry journey, the squeaky wheel gets the grease. In other words, needy (or call them greedy), immature congregants tend to clamor for your attention, making boundaries sometimes challenging.

Coping with Chaos

When my husband and I made the transition from youth pastors to lead pastors, we quickly discovered a new level of crazy. Maybe it's not true for all ministers, but it was certainly true for us! The first six months felt like we had suddenly opened a counseling center, instead of leading a church. The calls started coming in and never seemed to let up. I had also enrolled in the social work program in college so my "helping" radar may have been too stimulated. Either way, it was consuming.

There was a constant flow of people who *needed to talk*—I'm sure you are familiar with that phrase—with either him or me. Some of you have already discovered that dreaded feeling you get when a person comes up to you after Sunday service and asks, "*Do you have time to get together?*" I was a full-time mother, pastor, and part-time student, and it felt as though we walked around in a fog. We put out one fire after another and looked at each other at the end of the day wondering where all our time had gone. I sometimes wonder if the congregation doesn't play a part in this. Maybe the desire to get wisdom from a fresh pastor for all of life's problems is a strong motivator? Whatever the case, we discovered quickly that there were those in the congregation that personally enjoyed having all our attention and we needed to do something about it.

My husband is a patient man who believes strongly in giving people the benefit of the doubt. I, on the other hand, having spent much of my working past in the insurance industry dealing with less-than-savory claimants, struggled to trust people, *or* their motives. We both needed each other in this situation. It's the beauty of a team: we both needed each other to keep ourselves balanced in this situation. He needed my discernment, and I needed his compassion and trust.

Our personal epiphany that change needed to happen came in the middle of the night as I sat in my living room listening to a woman who had monopolized our time for hours saying nothing, absolutely nothing. She had called about eleven p.m. in a crisis, claiming to desperately be in need of our counsel for her struggles. When three a.m. hit, something in both of us snapped. As a mother of small children, sleep was important and we were getting nowhere fast. She was a control-freak of sorts who talked a great talk, but displayed rotten fruit in her walk. She had been a leader and an influential woman in the church (on the surface), but her character and personal life was in shambles. I remember looking at my husband after she left and saying, "*Never again! Do not ask me to have another meeting with her again. I'm finished."* I didn't need to do much convincing; both of us had the same "AHA!" moment that night.

Here is an unfortunate reality. There are those in the body who will distract us from doing what Christ wants us to do. Whether or not they are conscious of their neediness or monopolizing manner doesn't really matter, we must learn to distinguish between helping and being manipulated. Make no mistake, it is not easy. There were contentious moments as her tentacles were slowly unwrapped from the church, and our lives. It took us about a year to get to the place where we realized we could either spend our ministry lives talking about each and every *concern* she was having at the moment, or we could get down to the business of mentoring believers who were willing and hungry to make an impact for Christ.

We discovered quickly that when we sought the Lord for His protection and wisdom in each situation, and did our part by setting healthy boundaries, God usually did the dirty work of moving people and their drama out of the center of our lives and church gracefully. We, as leaders, need to prioritize the Great Commission. If we don't do it, neither will our congregation. If we have to move around people who only want to challenge, instead of change, do it. We know that God has prioritized the Great Commission and in ministry, we want to be on *His* side. He will need to take care of those who are not interested in His priorities. So we began quickly putting together strategies for healthy boundaries for ourselves. I would like to share a few of the most important ones with you. Here's where we started:

- Define and discern what is a true emergency;
- If I'm working harder than they are, something must change;
- Prioritize those people who want to grow and be led deeper in their walk with Christ your priority; some people don't want to be happy
- I don't have to answer the phone every time it rings;

- Outside, professional counseling is sometimes necessary and suggested;
- Pre-screen individual requests to "meet" with you

These boundaries quickly brought our time management back into place and put the power for our time back into our hands. It helped eliminate those spiritually narcissistic people who were distracting us from our role as shepherds. Let's talk about each of them in more detail.

What is a True Emergency?

First, be able to quickly identify whether you are dealing with a true emergency. This may be difficult in the initial phase of getting to know a person. However, it's good (and not rude) to ask questions when people call, even if they are highly emotional. One of you needs to be calm and rational.

Some good questions: *Where are you now?* (If they are in a hospital, police station, or funeral home, these are good indicators that it is a true emergency!) *Who are you with? Is there someone there that can pray with you?* It's important for people to realize that other believers in the Body of Christ can pray for each other. They do not need only a pastor to pray for them. I know this can be more difficult in smaller churches where the pastor or spouse is expected to run to the hospital for every occasion of illness or injury.

If this is the case at your church, start slowly—but begin immediately—teaching and empowering your people to do ministry in the body of Christ. This may take a great deal of time to reteach, but it is a worthy investment of your time. Help them to see that you cannot do it all and remain healthy. If you are not healthy, they are not healthy. You may lose a few in the process who refuse to let go of "pastor codependency," but I question how much fruit they are producing in your church anyway. We have over the years empowered a strong group of church members who will go and do prayer ministry when someone is sick or in the hospital. It really is a beautiful thing to see in action as relationships and community develops.

If I sense a person is simply demanding my time, and this particular situation is not a true emergency that would warrant my family missing out on another night away from me, I might limit my actions to emergency prayer on the phone and schedule a follow-up for a later date. It sounds like this: "*Wow, I can see how this has impacted you. Do you mind if I pray with you right now over the phone? I can't get away right now, but I would love to take a moment and pray together.*" Sincerity matters here. People can sense when you are trying to get rid of them.

I think it's so important to value those individual who *are* needy but still maintain good boundaries. I love them and have asked God over the years to help me love them enough to be strong when they are not. I love them enough to teach them to not take advantage of people or be demanding. Love does not demand its own way. I love them enough to ensure that they have a healthy pastor and pastor's wife who have time to hear from God on their behalf and grow them up into a strong, mature believer. I also love my pastor enough to want to ensure that he has a healthy marriage and family. It matters to them that I have a healthy marriage. It matters to them that our relationship with Jesus is passionately stirred. That must be our heart for these individuals. You can value them by speaking to them with gentleness, respect, *and* honesty. Be real about your time and make sure you keep God's priorities as your priorities.

On the flip side, if it is a true emergency, then make it your emergency. Don't negate your leadership responsibility when it matters. Though not often convenient, it is a privilege to be invited into people's lives during their most difficult seasons. Our care and attention to them during those times communicate our love for them.

As I look back over the years, I am amazed at the ministry opportunities God has given us during people's emergencies. My husband has had the privilege to preach the gospel at the funeral service of a teen girl who was tragically murdered in our community. We have opened our home for people seeking safety because of domestic violence issues. We have sat with broken people who have hit rock bottom and finally, see no other option but Jesus. I have been privileged to speak at the funeral of a beautiful little girl, Moriah, who brightened our church and taught us so much in just a short time about what is important in life.

Even as I write this section, I just received a note from a beautiful lady in my congregation who has been diagnosed with cancer and is terribly frightened. My heart aches for her and yet at the same time, I realize it is for this moment that God has placed us in her life. I pray that we can be strong, so she has spiritual and emotional strength to lean on as she walks this road. No one should walk alone and God has given us a great privilege and opportunity. Take those opportunities that He places in front of you willingly, and joyfully, even in the midst of pain, so He can freely use you and work in the lives of people.

How Hard Are You Working?

Next, you must evaluate who is working harder in the relationship. I have found that people can think it chic to be mentored by the pastor or pastor's wife. Having hung around myself for a long time, I'm not really sure why this is the case! Some days I feel anything but chic. But some people feel important if they are close to leadership.

Over the years, I have carefully prayed over those girls and ladies I saw that were eager and motivated to grow through my mentorship. It came after learning the hard way. If you are meeting with someone on a regular basis, you should have goals and action steps for that person to work on. Even the best counselor or mentor will feel trapped if there is no growth or goal in sight.

What are the goals? What action steps are necessary to get there? If things are not changing, ask yourself who is working harder? I have found that if I am doing most of the work, I am trying to force change upon people who are not invested. If they are not invested, change will become external and legalistic and everyone will be miserable. Here are some good questions:

- *"What do you see that needs to happen for this situation to change?"*
- *"Are you willing to do what it takes?"*
- *"I can't do this for you. You must be willing to take the steps necessary to make changes, so it's important to have goals. How do you feel about this?"*

When they call you to meet again, ask them if they have done those things you came up with at your last meeting together. If not, carefully and gently let them know that meetings that don't produce fruit are a waste of time for both of you.

Some people are only in need of a friend. While you will be a friend to most in your congregation, you can't be the confidante and mentor for each and every one of them. You must, carefully and prayerfully, select those people you mentor or disciple. As a shepherd, this is your responsibility. Encourage them to get involved in small groups, fellowship opportunities, etc. It might sound like this: *"It sounds like you need a good friend to go through life with and that is very important to each of us. We all need this. Can I encourage you to give our Connect group system a try to help you build friendships within the body of Christ?"*

My goal is to give you a practical application to how to do this gently. Please apply your own style that reflects genuine love and respect. Here is a secret I will share with you: *I love to play matchmaker.* My husband, on the other hand, does not like me to play matchmaker. He sees it as meddling (which it is), but I have a difficult time putting it to rest. So these instances are great opportunities for me to play matchmaker-*in a positive way*-by by connecting people for the purpose of building friendships that will help people grow *and* give them a healthy support system.

Unfortunately, one sad fact of ministry is not everyone is willing to grow up. I believe it's important to learn to quickly recognize who those people are and minimize your time dealing with them. This may take some time to figure out. I've poured many hours into people before seeing this, so don't feel bad when you feel you've "wasted" your time. I don't believe any lesson is wasted before the

Lord. He will honor our efforts by sharpening us as individuals and leaders in the process, despite someone else's refusal to mature.

There were many years in the beginning of our pastorate that I worked hard to make sure I was well liked. As I've mentioned earlier, I had a real need to please people. This was a pride issue for me because of my fear over what others thought of me.

Unfortunately, the fruit of people-pleasing is usually resentment, which constricts your freedom to love. My pride kept me imprisoned to fear and I secretly began to resent our church people because no matter what I did, I couldn't make everyone happy. When someone left, I found myself taking it personal and letting it intimidate me even more into that prison of pressure. This also made it really difficult to love to them.

I think being a shepherd is a lot like being a parent. The best parenting is done when motivated by love. When we parent out of fear, guilt, or ego, there will be sick and twisted results. Do you know that God wants you to genuinely love your congregation? You can't do this without Him, though. It is only through His grace that He can free you from the fear of what others think, and give you *His* heart for them. Make that your prayer—and then, begin to release yourself from the need to please people. I will share my personal testimony of this in a later chapter.

When it is all said and done, you will stand before your Lord and it matters most what *He* thought of our ministry and our lives. Paul reflects his own motivation in preaching the gospel to the church of Galatia, *"Am I now trying to win the approval of men, or of God? Or am I trying to please men? If I were still trying to please men, I would not be a servant of Christ."* (Gal. 1:10) If you are trying to please people, you, ultimately, become their slave, instead of their shepherd. While you are there to serve the church, the desire to please them cannot be your master. You must be mastered by the One who gives you the vision to lead, and the ability to love. This motivation will keep your heart in a state to continually receive from the Lord the grace needed to pastor your church.

Learning to Unplug

This next one is easy: *you don't need to answer your phone every time it rings!* With texting and cell phones, we've bought into the lie that we must be available 24 hours a day to people. I see this especially with the younger generation. Somewhere it was taught that it is rude to not respond immediately when someone texts you. The question that you have to ask is this: w*ho is accountable to God for your time?* You are. You should, then, have the authority to make the call (no pun intended) when you can and cannot communicate with people.

I've gotten better at this since I've been homeschooling my children. Many people don't realize the profound time it takes to teach my kids at home. It is a full-time job and the time during the day belongs to them because they are my priority, as is their education. I've made it clear that when I am schooling my kids, I can't talk and I rarely schedule appointments during this time. It is no easy task, so I guard intrusions into this time very carefully.

Your personal time with the Lord and family life is also a top priority. Ultimately, you are responsible for how well you guard the time needed to nurture these relationships. You must give yourself the freedom to step away from all of the burdens of church life, to minister to yourself and your family. If you aren't healthy, how can you lead? If it is a true emergency, they will leave a message.

I frequently check my messages or texts, and step back into my role as pastor's wife, if it truly is an emergency. Sometimes when I get more urgent texts, I respond with *"Can't talk right now…I will call you once I'm free."* I've had to learn to resist the pressure of justifying myself when I can't be available to people; most people don't want to know, or need to know, how I manage my time.

I have discovered another boundary that is becoming increasingly important when it comes to technology: *taking regular breaks from social media.* There are days where I truly feel ruled by so many distractions of technology that I can't focus. Chalk this up to middle-age or the technology-age; it doesn't matter, I have to find ways to recalibrate my mental abilities.

So I have recently instituted a Sabbath or fast from technology on a weekly basis. This has helped me turn off the distractions and voices that tend to drown out the voice of the Lord. Have you ever reached a place where you can't take another opinion? This is my red flag that I better unplug soon or my compassion will hit a new low! The enemy will not hesitate to distract us from time spent in prayer and intercession, study of God's Word, and rest, in general. Sometimes we don't need another "app" to be more efficient. We need to shut off all the other "apps" that are running in our heads, so we can recharge and think more clearly.

Outsource Big Issues

This next boundary is really important. Some people come to Christ with extensive baggage and helping them can be consuming. I've learned that it's important to remember that I am not a savior. When it comes to very difficult situations, I find it may be in their best interest (and mine) to refer them to a professional, godly counselor.

How do you know best when to do this? Following are some examples where my husband or I might refer a person for counseling.

- **If a person's issues are debilitating, or profoundly impacting their life.** This may be an instance where they need more urgent, frequent counseling than a pastor or pastor's wife can provide.
- **If outside expertise is helpful or necessary.** If you find yourself in certain situations that you are not familiar with such as eating disorders, addiction, sexual abuse, etc.
- **If the person is suicidal, homicidal, or otherwise, becoming dangerous**. Connect them immediately to a professional who can get them the appropriate care. You may also need to contact the proper authorities, if there is immediate danger. Don't bear this burden alone. One night I received a phone call from a pastor in another town. One of his parishioners had relocated to our town and found

herself entangled in a domestic violence situation. He called asking for our help. I did what any good pastor's wife should do. I took down all the information, ended the call, and then, dialed 9-1-1. I relayed the information, and people who were qualified to walk into volatile, dangerous situations went in and checked it out. We need to guard ourselves from stupid situations and not try to be a hero. How can we best serve the person and the situation? Sometimes it is best to let the authorities handle things when emotions are high and come in afterwards to help the person put the pieces back together.

- **If you find yourself counseling, more than mentoring, the person into spiritual maturity.** As I mentioned before, some people are looking for a listening ear, more than they are looking to change. You can't counsel too many people weekly or you will not have time to lead your church. Other people go into ministry to counsel, so let them counsel. It's okay to give yourself permission to refer in these situations.
- **If you are simply overrun with counseling appointments.** A tired, overwhelmed pastor or pastor's wife is rarely going to be helpful. Recognize your limitations! I am a morning person. If you want the best wisdom from me, meet me at 6:00 a.m. for coffee. I will be filled with great ideas and inspiring wisdom! However, if you call me after 8:00 p.m., you will be lucky if I am coherent enough to put sentences together. My ministry team has learned this fact, and rarely calls late at night for advice. Be willing to admit your weaknesses. I find that most people are grateful when I am honest about those limitations. It shows you care enough about them, to do what is best for them.

Good counselors can be hard to find so it requires you to do your homework when making counseling referrals. It may mean taking a counselor to lunch to get a handle on their ideology. Every

Christian label is not equal in the counseling world. As a social worker, I recognize this. I have also discovered that many go into counseling because they were helped by someone. Though the motive is good, the counselor should have the mark of good fruit in their life before they can help someone else. Serving out of own personal pain can be dangerous. Nevertheless, you have to sometimes make a judgment call when someone needs more than just pastoral counseling.

My husband and I have also benefited from "cleansing" ministries in our church for those people who need to walk through more intense discipleship and healing. If you don't have one, it may be worth the investment to build a ministry of healthy, mature believers to help you put this together.

Ask Good Questions

Finally, when people ask to meet with you, learn to ask them some questions. My husband taught me this, and it has been tremendously helpful. Ask them questions to find out what they are seeking from you. This is not rude (unless you are rude in how you ask), but helpful in clarifying that you are the right person to meet with them.

It helps in two ways: 1) it helps you to begin to pray and seek God for wisdom with the situation in helping them; and 2) you can weed through the requests that can be handled without the need for an outside meeting. Some people suggest a meeting out of respect for my time at church. They recognize that Sundays are usually pretty crazy with non-stop ministry. I appreciate that greatly. However, I have found that by asking good questions, it can sometimes be resolved immediately with a quick chat and prayer.

It also helps in the situations where they would be more appropriately served by another staff member (e.g. if it involves their ministry). My time away from my family (especially at night) needs to be carefully guarded, so I look for ways to avoid another trip into the church and away from family. I also find that sometimes I can schedule my meetings before or after a church activity to minimize those trips and outside appointments.

We have also found that sometimes well-meaning people will come to us to fix—*there's that word again*— their friends and family members. It may be a mother who is worried about her child and wants us to call him. It may be a wife who wants someone to talk to her unbelieving husband so she comes to us for help. Occasionally, this works out into a ministry opportunity; but, mostly, it just creates awkward conversations.

When approached, I tell the person that I would be more than happy to talk to anyone about Jesus or life, if they are willing. What shows me they are willing is their willingness to contact me. Put the ball in their court. Again, this is my personal opinion on this type of situation. I like to give permission for this worried or troubled person to give out my contact information with the suggestion that the person contact me directly. It saves you chasing people who are not interested in talking to you. Well-meaning people are not always led by the Holy Spirit, but by guilt or desperation. Be available, but let God open the doors of a person's heart so you aren't doing more harm than good.

Another thing that happens frequently in ministry is triangulation. Sometimes people perceive the pastor's wife as "easier" to approach and so they bring their troubles with staff or my spouse to me. This creates a triangle in the relationship between three people that is not healthy.

First, I can't solve the problem. Second, it is unfair for me to answer for another staff member's actions. Third, it is not biblical. It is best in these cases where someone complains or brings a problem to you about staff or your spouse to refer them back to that person immediately and offer to connect them personally. If a person has poor motives here, he or she will usually back out of this quickly. If the motives are pure, you can connect them to the real person who can resolve the issue or bring reconciliation.

Having good, healthy boundaries is pivotal to thriving and finding joy in ministry. Invest your time and energy wisely into a team that you can empower to help you carry the load.

Over the years, I've narrowed my mentoring down to my staff pastors' wives, women's ministry leaders, and a few other ladies to whom I've felt called to be a "spiritual mother". You cannot counsel or mentor *every* person who asks. Some people do not want to grow. Some are only curious about you and your life. Don't mistake the requests of people as a responsibility to be everyone's savior. Keep your heart and home healthy. You're going to need to be healthy when you hit those bumps ahead on the ministry road.

Chapter 6

Help! I'm Married to the Pastor!

One of the greatest gifts you can give your congregation is a healthy marriage. In this day of heated debates over the sacredness of marriage, the church needs to be about the business of not just "talking" about God's design for sacred marriage, but proving it works best with their own lives. Unfortunately, this is missing from most churches today. Sad to say, I have observed that it is missing from too many ministry families as well.

I recently met with a pastor's wife who was struggling to support her husband. He had ventured into the ministry world like so many others without waiting on his wife to be at peace with this brand new idea, and he was reaping the unfortunate results.

While she wasn't bitter, she *was* apathetic about ministry. She just wasn't sure how to jump on board with him because he had never waited for her to be committed and she struggled with the call and where she fit in. Needless to say, he was serving on his own and she was nowhere to be seen. This doesn't work for too long and is a miserable place for both.

With so many demands on our time from both children and congregations, it is easy to let our marriage take a back seat. It will be to the detriment of our family and church, if we fail to protect our marriages.

So what can a pastor's wife do to invest in her marriage? Though Proverbs 31 gets a bad rap, it's a good idea to look there for guidance in how to be a good wife!

"A wife of noble character who can find? She is worth more than rubies. Her husband has full confidence in her and lacks nothing of value. She brings him good, not harm all the days of her life."
(Proverbs 31:10-12).

While this book does not permit me space to cover all aspects of marriage, I want to talk about the unique challenges ministry brings to marriage. This scripture in Proverbs speaks to the value of having a wife who is not just on the same team as her husband, but one who invested in her marriage and is an asset to her husband. As a result, she is enjoying the fruit of that investment.

Whatever we feed grows, and I can honestly say the best fruit in my life has come from making my marriage a priority. I have enjoyed the benefits and joys of a healthy and intimate marriage. That is the heart of God for each of you. Together, you and your spouse can achieve more than if you try to do it on your own!

Foundationally, here are a few of the simple things I've learned over the years that might help you as seek to love your husband well and protect your marriage in the process:

- Make him a priority with your time and attention;
- Cover and protect him;
- Inspire, help, and believe in his dreams;
- Intercede for him daily.

I remember when I read my first book on being a godly wife. I don't remember the name of that book, but I do remember reading something that provoked great fear into my Type-A perfectionistic heart. The author mentioned that every day she asked her husband if there was something she could do to help him that day. Then, she went on to suggest that her readers should do the same.

I can't describe the sheer terror that struck my heart at that suggestion. Didn't she know how busy I was? My to-do list as a wife, mother, pastor's wife, *and* (at that time) an insurance adjuster working full-time was already too long! I really struggled to take that suggestion to heart.

I remember clearly the day I finally took the step of faith. I sat down next to my husband, looked at him, cringed, and with a deep breath quickly threw out these words, *"Is there anything I can do today to help you?"* I closed my eyes and waited for the bomb to drop. He just stared at me. I'm not sure what was running through his mind, but he obviously thought it was humorous judging from the smile he was trying to hide. He knew how hard this was for me and was really enjoying the moment!

Needless to say, it was much less painful than expected. I don't even know what his request was. He may not have even had one! But what mattered was that he seemed genuinely pleased at the idea that I would think enough of him to ask. Even if it was a cautious, reluctant, request!

Paying Attention to What's Important

So let's start with the basics. *Does your husband have any of your time and attention?* This was a tough one for me because from the time I get up in the morning until I fall into bed at night, my mind is racing with things to do. My intense personality makes me slightly unbearable at times, but my husband has been very patient with helping me in this area.

Like so many other women, I spent so many of our early marriage years *doing* for my husband that I didn't realize that I wasn't really listening to him or paying attention to what he really needed. I felt that caring for our babies, working in the church, and doing all the grocery shopping was enough for him to feel like a priority. I was wrong. I spent those years doing things according to my love language (acts of service) before I realized that he interprets love through words of affirmation and quality time (of course, my most difficult). What a wake-up call that was to me!

At first, I was a bit resentful because I thought, *"It's the thought that counts!"* My motivation is important, but motivation alone doesn't nurture a marriage or intimacy. The more I listened to my husband—and set aside my pride—the more I realized what he needed was not all that difficult; it was just *different* from what I had thought. Here I was back at this issue of change! But this change mattered, and it was worth stopping and reassessing what love is really all about.

Take the time to find out what speaks love to your husband. It matters! Ask him and don't react negatively to his response. I know this can be hard. The point is that the two of you are in this thing called ministry together, and you need each other to be successful and grow. Your investment in making him a priority will pay great dividends in your marriage, your ministry, and your family.

One other thing I should mention. The greatest gift you can give your kids is a solid investment in your marriage. Sometimes as moms we think the sacrifice and care of our children should be our top priority. This is not biblical. Our relationship with God is first, our husband is second, and our children are third. Is God being unfair to our children? No, it's quite the opposite. He is ensuring that your children are safely protected and nurtured in a home that is secure and loving with two parents modeling a picture of sacred love. That is priceless and better than any gift you can give your kids with your time or money.

Cover and Protect

My next question is this, *"Does your husband have your protection?"* At first, this may seem like a strange question because usually the husband is seen as the protector in the marriage relationship. But there is high value assigned in Proverbs 31 to the woman who brings good, and not harm, to her husband.

How does this work? I believe that the wife of the pastor has a great responsibility to protect and cover her husband with a fierce and loving loyalty. Please don't misunderstand what I am saying when I use the words *"cover"* and *"protect"*. I am not referring to covering-up sin or corruption, but covering him so that he can be most effective in proclaiming the gospel. Let me explain.

The Proverbs 31 woman demonstrates so many ways that a woman can honor the Lord with her life. While few women have all of these attributes, we should want to be women whose lives bring glory to God. We should want to make a difference doing well. I love this quote from author, Ann Voskamp: *"You get to decide whether you're going to spend your one life trying to make an impression and look good—or make a difference and do good."* So what will we do with the life we have been given?

We can secretly resent and feel intimidated by the life that the Proverbs 31 woman lived, *or* we can see the possibilities she inspires in each of us to contribute and use whatever we have in our hand. If you are reading this book, you have a pastor/husband that God has given you. What an opportunity to bring good to the man you love and with whom you have partnered your life and ministry!

The Proverbs 31 wife was trusted to do good to her husband. This does not only mean *doing* good things but *bringing* him good so he has full confidence in her to protect him. This means she can be trusted with the finances of the family. She isn't running them into financial ruin with out-of-control spending.

She can be trusted to bring good to his name by her behavior. She isn't acting improperly, immodestly, or immorally, and bringing shame to the family. She can be trusted to raise her children in a godly manner because she is committed to Jesus first, and knows how vital it is for her kids to love Jesus.

She can be trusted to protect his role of pastor in the church. Her love for the church and commitment to the gospel keeps her from acting rashly or in a manner that brings dishonor to that gospel. These are hard but necessary things that communicate love to your pastor.

I wish I could tell you I've always had this figured out, but I haven't. For many of our early years in ministry, I didn't understand the importance of protecting. I must confess that I sometimes used my husband along with my sarcastic sense of humor to make others laugh. Sometimes, I let my strong-willed heart cause problems as I resisted or demeaned his decisions or actions in front of our children. Then one day the Lord spoke to me about the manner in which I represented Carey to others, especially the church and my children.

1 Corinthians 13:7 tells us that love always protects. I was not protecting his role as father in their eyes. I began to see the impact my responses were having on my children. They were becoming disrespectful in their responses to him and increasingly dismissive of his requests. I realized then the damage I was doing and I repented, feeling broken-hearted that I would do this to the man I claimed to love and to whom I had committed my life.

Additionally, the Lord began to wake me to the reality that my husband was the primary communicator of the gospel in my church. If I spoke poorly or complained about him to our people all week long, I could expect on Sunday it would be difficult for them to see past "the man" I had portrayed in my witty moment and receive the Word. I didn't want to make anything a stumbling block for people needing to receive the transforming truth of the gospel. It was a humbling moment.

Even in fun, be careful of the comments you throw out to people about their pastor. It may become a stumbling block to that person's ability to respect and receive from him. Again, I am not advocating covering up sinful behavior. On the contrary as much as love protects, it must also seek the higher good of each other. So, if there is sin, it should be dealt with, but we cover and protect the honor of his role as husband, father, and pastor.

Don't Stop Believing

I admit it. I was raised in the eighties. It was a time of big hair and shallow music. In spite of my church upbringing, I grew up listening to the secular bands of that time period. Journey's overnight hit song, *"Don't Stop Believing"* was one of my favorite songs during that era. Now I realize the overall message of the song was not exactly uplifting, but it stirred something inside of us as a generation. It stirred our hearts for more, for something worthwhile, in our hunt for an emotion, for love, for something that really mattered. I believe that hope is a distinguishing characteristic that separates humanity from all other creation. No matter what tragedies or circumstances come our way, we all as humans crave to do something that matters in the end.

One day I realized that my husband, too, is human. I know you may be thinking right about now that I am a little slow. Carey would tell you that I am just a little too preoccupied at times, so I miss the little things, especially the things that mattered to my husband. Just like me, he has dreams, desires, and a vision that he believes God wants him to fulfill.

What about you? Are you aware of your husband's dreams? Does your husband know that you believe in him? Does he really believe that you believe in him? It's so easy to say it, but our actions speak louder than our words.

One of the great questions of the man's heart is this: *Do I have what it takes?* It took some time into our marriage before I realized how important it was that I inspire my husband to believe that he does have what it takes (through Christ) to lead our family and our church well. Pastors face a great deal of intimidation and many voices tearing them down and telling them quite the opposite! What are you telling him with your actions? Do you pay lip-service to his dreams and then write them off as silly? Or do you listen to him and dialogue with him to help him put feet to those dreams?

Can I be honest? This is very hard for me as I am not a woman who inspires by nature. Quite the opposite, I have a tendency to interpret things negatively and see the glass as always half-empty. When I began to study in the Word what it means to be an inspirer, I became fascinated at the power that God has given the wife to help her husband lead their family.

If you don't see this, just spend a few minutes observing a young man who has recently fallen in love. What do you observe? This young man has stopped eating (*a miracle in itself*), thinking, or playing. All he can do is think of *her*. It's as if someone has taken his brain captive and he can no longer think.

One of Carey's favorite movies is *Rocky*. He loves the part where Rocky has hit bottom with everything in his life falling apart.

At that perfect moment, his wife, Adrian awakens from her coma to inspire Rocky to, *"Win!"*

These aren't just silly things we put in movies without reason. They resonate with the audiences because people, especially men, are looking for a reason, or a cause, to rise up and meet. We need someone to inspire us to keep going. I believe God has placed a husband and wife together for good reason. I was surprised how much it mattered to Carey what I thought about his ability to succeed in life.

Proverbs 14:1 says *"The wise woman builds her house but with her own hands the foolish one tears hers down.* Have you ever heard the phrase: *"If momma ain't happy, nobody is happy?"* Why do we say this? Because it's true!

For a few years, I tried to ignore that phrase because it created a sense of guilt and responsibility that I didn't like. Eventually the Lord really revealed how I have been given the power of my femininity to impact the atmosphere in my home. I was impacting it whether I realized it or not. Unfortunately, I was mostly impacting it negatively with my moodiness. My husband and kids walked around on eggshells whenever I was in a foul mood. It really bugged me that I couldn't just be grumpy without feeling like everyone else was affected by my grumpiness. God, in His great faithfulness, broke through my stubborn will and helped me to see the *opportunity* I had to direct the atmosphere in my home and life. What a changing moment that was for all of us!

God has given us this great power as a help to our spouse and those we encounter all around us. Adam was not in need of just a companion, God knew he needed *help.* Your spouse needs you in his life. Both of you are necessary to help the other become better and more like Christ. Living with each other should be great proof of that! Quite honestly, sometimes the challenges of ministry can take a toll on that belief. You have within your grasp the ability to help or hurt your spouse with that influence; the power to believe and achieve the vision God has given your family.

Our power to inspire was not given to us as a destructive, controlling tool for our own pleasure and self-gratification, or even to manipulate those that we love. Rather, it was meant to be a gift wielded with love to build up those people around us—those that we have been give the responsibility to inspire. I know God has called me to inspire my husband, my kids, my church, and anyone else I have an opportunity to inspire. This insight forced me shift my idea of what it meant to be a *helpmate.* I used to despise that word because it felt like such a dull, uninteresting, word. Do you know what I mean? Maybe I secretly feared it would make me dull and uninteresting. Quite the contrary, I find that it has drawn others, especially my husband, closer to me. God has entrusted us with a great responsibility and opportunity that we need to take seriously.

What kind of wind are you blowing into the sails of your marriage and family? How about your church and neighborhood? Lay your fears and faulty ideas aside. Take a risk to raise the sails and don't stop believing where God will take you.

Powerful and Effective—or Not

Finally, the most important work that you can do to show love for your husband is to pray for him. This is said so often that I almost hate to write it. It just becomes something we check off our list without giving it much thought or time.

James 5:16 stresses the power of praying for each other: "*Therefore confess your sins to each other and pray for each other so that you may be healed. The prayer of a righteous woman* (my personalized version) *is powerful and effective.*" I bet that many of us can quote this verse and tell our church members why they should be praying according to this scripture.

Unfortunately, believing scripture and living scripture are two different things. I know this from experience. Years of Bible Quiz taught me the *knowledge*, but life by the Spirit has shown me how to *live it out.* If we really believed that our prayers made a difference in our husband's lives or ministry, I believe that we would spend more time praying and less time complaining. My tendency is to complain first and pray second. God is trying desperately to change this. He wants to teach us the power that praying right away can have in our lives and in our situations.

There is a scene in the third movie of *Lord of the Rings* that helps illustrate this. Ewoyn, the beautiful Rohan princess, in the thick of the battle with her countrymen, finds her precious uncle knocked to the ground by a large creature ridden by the supernatural, Witch King. As this dreadful creature seeks to devour the flesh of her king, she stands in front of his wounded body with her little sword in her hand, looks that giant in the eyes, and says with all the courage and passion, she can muster, "*I will kill you if you touch him!*" She proceeds to battle this evil using not masculinity, but fully embracing all her femininity.

God has given us the responsibility to be watchfully praying over our families and homes. I believe that a praying woman is a dangerous woman. A woman who is willing to do battle against the kingdom of darkness on behalf of the man she loves. Watching this scene was a spiritual moment for me. Do I have this same attitude as I do battle on my knees against the powers of darkness? Do I believe that my prayers make a life and death difference as I vigorously defend them in intercession with all that is within me?

My heart is that you realize how desperately your husband needs you to pray for him. There is a spiritual battle raging all around your husband, home, and church. I have become fully convinced that one of my most important roles as a wife and pastor's wife is to do dangerous battle on behalf of those I love.

What about you? Has not God gifted you with a feminine intuition that helps you know how and when to intercede for your husband? Are you willing to stand in the gap for those who need you to fight on their behalf? Your commitment to do this small, but powerfully effective, task on a daily basis conveys to your husband that you are *for* him. With so many against him in ministry, isn't it important that he knows you are making him a priority by praying for him? What would he dare to dream if he knew you would choose to partner with him through the difficult decisions and dreams with your intercession? Do you have enough faith to believe that you can make a difference through your prayers? I believe you do.

Fanning Those Flames

No chapter on marriage would be complete without including the topic of sex. As my husband says, *"Fire inside the fireplace is very good! Fire outside the fireplace is very bad!"*

My greatest words of wisdom to you are these: **cultivate a good fire inside the fireplace!** Let your husband know frequently that you desire him and spend time together fanning the fire. You both need the protection and pure enjoyment of a healthy sex life. This should only grow as you mature in your marriage relationship together.

I recall reading an article some years ago stressing that married couples should never let each other leave home "hungry." I think you understand the point. Sex is good. It is a gift from God given to two people committed to love each other and grow in intimacy together. If it's not good now, figure out what you need to do to make it better. Get healing for past hurts and insecurities. Put aside your pride or fear, and communicate what you need or desire.

Both of you should be receiving from each other and no other source. This includes emotional nurturing. As women, we are wired emotionally and can create emotional bonds outside of our marriage relationship that are dangerous. Run from private, emotionally-charged conversations with either the same-sex or the opposite-sex. I am very serious about this. It is possible to meet our emotional needs from someone else (man or woman) who is not your spouse without being sexually unfaithful in the physical sense. But it can lead to a fire outside of the fireplace in a hurry.

Even friendships, over time, can deteriorate the special, private relationship between husband and wife if we are not careful. Marriage is a covenant relationship made before God to make your spouse your first priority. Keep others out of the top spot in your heart including kids, friends, coworkers, and especially, mothers!

A Special Note to the Hurting Pastor's Wife

Finally, let me conclude this chapter on a more serious note. This chapter is obviously directed to you, the pastor's wife, to help you see the opportunity you have to love and strengthen your marriage. However, I realize that just because a man is in ministry does not necessarily mean he is meeting the needs of his wife or family. Unfortunately, the reality of selfishness, anger, past hurts, or simply the busyness of life may continually encroach upon your marriage and create distance, problems, and yes, sometimes even crisis. I've discovered that some men really don't know how to blossom a woman; rather than cultivate beauty, they crush her spirit with apathy, neglect, or harshness. (More on this in chapter 12.)

Too often, the pastor and his wife stay silent and miserable in their marriage for too long out of fear. Many stay quiet out of a fear of being exposed as failures, or fear of being fired from ministry positions. In very few other vocations does the failure of your marriage mean the end of your career and income, as it does for those of us who serve in ministry. This is hard reality. By the time a crisis hits and you are willing to go public, many marriage partners have emotionally detached or stopped believing any longer that there is hope to save the marriage.

May I encourage you to lay aside your pride or fear and reach out for help? It matters to your congregation what kind of marriage you have. It matters to your children. As followers of Christ, we don't have the luxury of compartmentalizing our lives.

Don't wait until things go too far before you do *your* part to make your marriage stronger. There is too much at stake. It is better to admit we are in need of grace before we give up and throw everything away. The truth is we all are in constant need of grace anyway. Even if your spouse resists or rejects the need for help, you find help. There are safe resources for those in ministry who need help, but it takes our willingness to ask for it. Contact a ministry friend, or leader, and reach out to someone to walk beside you during these difficult days, before it is too late.

One last thing. I know it can sometimes be scary to put yourself out emotionally, even in a godly marriage. It was terrifying for me at first. My early years of emotional hurt created great insecurities inside my heart. The fear of being unsafe in a man's hands runs deep.

So I did something different: I chose instead to place my heart into God's capable hands. I have found when God is the holder of my heart He keeps it safely guarded in His hands. My gift of love and submission to my husband is really not about my husband. It's about a life sacrificially poured out as worship to God. When I love my husband, I am worshiping God with a sacrifice and it helps to keep my motivation in the right place.

God will care for you and your needs until your husband changes. It may be that He will use *you* to help bring about the change your spouse needs to become more like Christ. In the meantime, become the woman He created you to be. You and your marriage will never regret it. May God continually increase your faith and give you grace while you love your pastor!

Chapter 7

Help! My Kids Are Not Perfect!

Becoming a mom was one of the greatest events of my life. I cannot think of any other single event that taught me God's deep love for His children, more than having my own children.

I have been blessed four times. I have a boy and a girl given to me biologically, and I have a boy and a girl given to me through the blessing of adoption. Each of my children is special, and likewise each has taught me something deeper about God and His love for us.

I think that raising kids—or more specifically, raising kids well—is one of the hardest jobs out there. Even harder than serving in ministry, raising your children to love God and love others is an enormous task not for the faint of heart. I have made so many mistakes in this process that I think this is the most humbling chapter to write.

When you become a parent, you suddenly gain the perspective that you really don't have control over everything. Ultimately, they get to choose. Everything. As a former control freak, sometimes that terrifies me! My oldest is now nineteen years old.

As I look back to when I began the journey, I am amazed how God has refined and chiseled my character so greatly through this process of parenting. While there were a few years of crisis during the early adoption years (coming in another chapter), my kids are really wonderful kids. Not perfect, just really wonderful.

Prepare for the Worse, Expect the Best

Obviously, raising kids in ministry has been a challenge. Overall, though, for us, it has been a positive experience. My kids love our church and they feel at home with our church family. They have been fortunate to have been in the same church their entire childhood. I realize other kids are not so lucky.

Some are bounced around every few years. Others are in very small churches with few children. And then there is the difficult transition—especially for the kids—of the transition from lay person to ministry position. Your kids are suddenly thrust into a new place of expectation and change.

If this is your scenario, it is going to be necessary to communicate with them often, and help walk them through this change. Sometimes it's tempting to take a more reactive approach of parenting them, instead. But if your kids are older, I recommend that you let your kids talk to other pastors and pastor's kids right away for a good picture of what to expect when you transition into ministry life. This will help them to know the challenges other pastor's kids are dealing with, so they know what and what not to take personally during the transition time. It also gives them the tools to navigate the journey and set realistic expectations.

We go into ministry sometimes with rose-colored glasses and great expectations. For the most part, it *is* a great experience. But what do you do when there are problems? Even worse, what do you do with the pain that sometimes comes to your kids? It's one kind of spiritual and emotional battle when the issues affect you and your husband. It's another kind of battle when your kids are involved. Especially as the mom, you must have a plan or you may find yourself reacting out of these emotions. You can't walk around going ballistic on people, although you may feel like it at times!

While there is a legitimate place for righteous anger, what matters most are the lessons you teach your children in those moments. I wish I could have shielded my kids from all of the pain of ministry and having parents who are pastors. All of us do. But I think that the Lord has taught them important lessons on how to handle disappointment and pain by watching us navigate through it.

I remember, one day, after we had been experiencing a mass exodus of people from our church with whom we had been very close. My oldest son and I were driving alone in the car. As we drove, he began to ask me questions about why a particular family left. My heart went to my throat. I breathed out a silent prayer and took a deep breath. I wasn't sure I could do it without falling apart.

Then I just began talking. Though I left out some of the messy details, I told him truthfully what was happening. He was old enough to understand. My husband and I try to present the facts of the situation without being overly critical of the people. This is no easy task when your own heart is bristling with pain and confusion. In fact, I must confess it is downright difficult, and at times I have had to go back to my kids and apologize for being harsh in a response or snide comment I've made about people. I have a tendency to be rather direct, so keeping a guard on my lips is forever a challenge.

One member of this particular family had been a friend of his. Not sure I was ready for his answer; I took a deep breath and asked the question, "*So, how are you doing with this*?" He looked at me and in a quiet voice said, *"I'm okay. I'm worried most about you, Mom. You've lost a good friend*." The tears flowed at this show of concern for *me*. It was not what I was expecting. I did my best to reassure him that I would heal from this one day and that God was caring for me in the process.

My heart broke that day as I realized how hard it must be for a child to watch other people hurt their parents. I was never a preacher's kid. I didn't really understand what he was going through. Yet I believe it's important to walk through pain in front of our kids in a very authentic way so they feel free to talk about it. While we don't break confidences, we should talk openly with them about the challenges of ministry, both the beauty and the heartache. It is our desire to raise kids who don't hate the ministry or church, in general. Too many kids walk away from God because of the actions of spiritually immature church members, or even worse, spiritually immature pastors. We can control hardly anything else, but we can control our own conduct and attitudes in the process for their good.

Lift Your Vision Higher

So how do we create an environment where our kids can thrive in ministry rather than die? I believe it starts with a foundational understanding of how families should operate biblically.

Just as God purposes His will in the lives of individuals, He also purposes His will in the family unit. Together with us, He desires to accomplish His will here on earth using the family—not just ministry families, but all families. So many people miss this important piece when leading and raising a family. That's why it is important to have a family vision.

What is God's vision for your family? What has He called you to do together that matters for eternity? This is something that you, as parents, have prayed through to guide, protect, and empower your family to accomplish His will together, and in each individual family member. We know He is working inside the family to make the individual members more like Christ, but He is also working in your family as a whole to do Kingdom work.

I know there are days when you don't see it this way, but your family is no mistake. It is not just a random accident! In fact, you need to see the beauty of how God specifically chose each one of your children just for you and your husband, and how He chose you and your husband, specifically, for each of your children. They needed you to be their parents, and you needed them to be your children. Maybe this doesn't make you feel better! However, this will help you when you go through the difficult times when you feel things are chaotic or too hard. Though it may sometimes feel like a punishment, it really is that God was thinking of what we would need in the long run to become more like Jesus.

Before you label yourself a failure as a parent, I think it's important to realize that God doesn't set people up to be failures, but to be conquerors. He sees things in us that we cannot possibly see in ourselves! The challenges and difficulties we face as parents will change us.

As I look at the tapestry that God has woven in my own family, I realize each one of my children (even when they were awful) were being used by Him to work things *in* or *out* of my life. Obviously, this required that I yield to what God was doing in the moment. I would not be the mom I am today, if not for the refining that God has worked in me through each of my children. Even though I sometimes grumble and complain, I am grateful for the change that has been wrought in me through the difficulties I have faced. And there have been many.

It's important to keep the right perspective. Look to God for a family vision that can direct your goals, actions, and dreams. You won't regret it.

Raising World Changers

Look at your child. Look at all your children. Do you see potential world changers? Maybe you do, but some days you may honestly wonder if they will ever just make it through grade school!

Whether you can see it or not, God desires to use each of your kids to bring about change in this world for His kingdom. He wants to use your family to impact the culture. And in case you haven't noticed, the culture is extremely toxic these days. God is working to increase the influence your family has on the world and culture around them, according to His will. I am raising world changers. I have no doubt about that.

Back when our kids were little, our family chose our very own confession (think of it like a mission statement) that went like this: *"The world does not revolve around me but was meant to be impacted by me."* Our kids started quoting this in kindergarten every morning before school and continued it through high school. When they acted selfishly, we would ask them to recite their confession, despite the eye rolling that occurred. Over and over, they said that confession. I didn't realize how this confession would challenge my trust and faith in God until the day came when my firstborn, Cal, graduated from high school.

Though this in itself was an emotional process, the real test of letting go came a couple months later when he boarded a plane to Northern Asia for an overseas mission internship. "*This cannot be happening!*" were my thoughts at the realization that I was placing my child on that plane bound for the other side of the world for the next 4 months. I struggled and my heart filled with fear as I sought the strength to keep it together long enough for him to get on that plane. "*Why can't I get it together? He is not dying!*" I muttered to my husband through my tears. "*It's really going to be ok. He will be back in four months,"* was his reassuring response.

I watched until there was nothing left to see as he walked up the ramp to the departing gate. I savored every second of the sight of him; then I turned as the sobbing hit me like a ton of bricks. My husband was not sure what to do with me. I was not sure what to do with me. Somehow I made my way through that airport and back to my car. I was fortunate to be driving home alone that day. It gave me some much needed privacy, a time for tears, *and* an emergency hearing before the Lord.

I began to beg, plead, and make demands of the Lord on that drive. If I was going to release my son to do Kingdom work, then I reminded the Lord that He needed to remember His end of the bargain, as if He would ever forget. It was a rough morning for this mom. After a long time of prayer, pleading, and tears, my mind went back to that moment at the airport watching him walk up that ramp for his plane. Quietly, the Lord began to whisper peace to my fear-filled heart.

As his mother, I felt forced to let go of my son, despite those seventeen years of nurturing and parenting. In fact, love compelled me to let him go. For him it would mean new places, new people, and new opportunities. Despite the reality of this wonderful opportunity, my heart was torn.

Then my mind began to think about a different moment in history where a Father surely agonized over the releasing of His firstborn Son for a mission altogether different than that of Cal. Like me, this Father was choosing to release His Son as a compulsion of love. But the future was not the same. His Son would walk a dark road. This Father would have to choose between His beloved Son and the crown of His creation. I don't know how He did it. As an omniscient Father, He knew the future that awaited His Son. They had been together eternally and now, as an act of love, He was releasing Jesus to a future of rejection, pain, and ultimately, a brutal death on a cross of sacrificial love.

In that quiet moment, I realized two things. First, that God truly understands our pain in loving and trusting our children to Him. He had endured a much greater pain than I was experiencing. It is difficult to let go of our kids, and it is also difficult to be at peace with the sometimes bumpy road that ministry life brings. The reality is, though, that our children are not ours to keep. They are God's first, and ours, second; and they were born to fulfill a destiny appointed by Him. To hold our kids back in fear, or selfishness, is not love at all.

The second truth I realized that morning was the overwhelming love God has for us. That He would care enough about us to release His Son and deal with the searing pain of a Father's heart to rescue all of humanity—*including my son*—was overwhelming. Who was I not to trust this kind of Father?

Suddenly, I experienced a great peace as the Scripture of 2 Timothy 1:12 flooded my soul, *"That is why I am suffering as I am. Yet I am not ashamed, because I know whom I have believed, and am convinced that he is able to guard what I have entrusted to him until that day."*

In the midst of my fear and sadness, I was fully convinced that those beautiful hands of God that released Jesus as an act of love could also be safely trusted to guard and protect *my* son as he journeyed around the world.

He gives us our children to prepare them to rise to the destiny of being world-changers. Unfortunately, that means they can't play it safe and sit on the sidelines. We get the joy of loving and caring for them, but they are not ours to hold back and protect. In all honesty, I would rather have my child cross the oceans and do dangerous work for Jesus than live down the street from me and not serve Jesus at all. Raise them to be world-changers and then entrust them to a trustworthy and loving Father!

Setting Them Up for Success

When we understand that God has put the family together to fulfill His purposes in each member, and in the world around us, we can begin to actively work together as a family serving in ministry.

If they hate the ministry, is it because they don't see themselves as part of it? Is it just a job that Dad does? Or is it something Mom and Dad do that keep them *away* from the kids, more often than they are *together*? This can happen if we separate our kids from playing a real part in our ministry.

Our family recently instituted a Friday evening prayer hour which includes a bit of family fun to start, and ends with prayer for our family, our church, and the nations. It has unified us so much as a family, and I believe it will produce great fruit in their lives.

We often remind our kids that we are a ministry family. If they struggle with it at times, we remind them it is not forever because, eventually, they will leave our family and find God's place for their family to begin to serve with a new vision, which may or may not include ministry, but will always include a holy destiny and family vision from God. Until that time, we teach them it is no mistake; they are exactly where God wants them to be to learn the things necessary to draw them closer to Him and become the man or woman He designed them to be.

In the early years when our kids were young, my husband and I often made a concerted effort to point out the perks of ministry to our kids. This was deliberate and especially important. If they got to go to a hotel for a conference with us, we would ask them, *"Do you know why you get to do this?"* Their answer came with shouts of joy, *"Because we are the pastor's kids!"* Yes, we encouraged them to be excited about those opportunities. This created a positive lens for them to view the ministry and it laid a solid foundation before they were old enough to be aware of the painful parts of ministry.

Help your kids connect the dots. Do you get special gifts at Christmas or a *"Pastor Appreciation Day?"* Before we celebrated and ate our goodies, we tried to remember to thank God, as a family, for the people who blessed us, and we celebrated our role as shepherds of a great church. I can't overstate the importance of this foundation. If you are struggling to see the privilege of shepherding people, maybe it's time to start thanking God for the people He has given you. Getting that mindset can be hard, especially if your heart has been wounded. It requires a little humble obedience and a large step of faith; don't overlook that. I promise you that God will faithfully respond to your risk of faith with great blessing.

When Troubles Come

No matter how wonderful your child is, or how wonderful your church is, eventually, he or she will hit a bump. Whether it is a simple misunderstanding, or something that was said in a goofy moment, it will come.

My first advice to you is this: *don't overreact.* Sometimes the bump comes during difficult seasons and it can feel like just another nail in the coffin. Be careful to evaluate the situation involving your kids on its own merit and not with all the other junk that is in the ministry "mix". Your child is not responsible for all the other problems, and overreacting will put up barriers between your child and ministry—or worse, between you and your child.

The other equally bad reaction is taking the defensive approach. Our children are human, and they need to be free to make mistakes so they can learn from them. Failure isn't fatal; it just proves that they are children. You are not a failure either. Guard yourself carefully from that pressure or you (and they) will be always angry. Defensiveness just pits the church people against the pastor's kid, and that is never a good place to be.

Teach your child how to react in humility and accept responsibility when they do something offensive or wrong. My youngest daughter is an "Anne Shirley" of sorts. She has a tendency to take over kid's church, if not properly led by the adult in charge. This has made for a few tense moments over the years during pick-up time on Sundays. When there is a bad report, she knows that she will need to go and apologize to the teacher. There are always many tears and emotions because she is highly dramatic and usually feels horrible after the fact. Nevertheless, we simply have to continue to hold her accountable. Our church family has been wonderful in helping us parent her sometimes strong, dramatic personality.

What about difficult people that like to pick on, or use your child? A few pictures of those people over the years just flashed into my head. They are in every church. They are people who have nothing else to do but evaluate your kids, or use them to fish for information.

I have a standard answer when someone comes "reporting" on my kids: "*That doesn't really surprise me. Thank you for telling me, I will discuss it with him or her.*" Notice I didn't try to explain anything to them. It's not their business. They were not given stewardship over our kids. Nor do I think it is right to give people power over our kids. That will only plant seeds of resentment in the hearts of our children. If the person had good motives, this is really the only answer they would expect anyway. If the motives were to make trouble, they don't need another answer. Obviously, if my kids have offended someone, then they need to go back and make it right.

When it comes to inquisitive people, my kids have a standard pat answer that they like to use if anyone tries to pull them into church drama or intrusive family questioning. *"Hmmm,* (an especially long 'Hmmm' gives them time to think before they answer) *I really don't know. You will need to talk to my parents about that."* Then they are instructed and empowered to walk away. They should never speak for, or defend their mom, dad, or any other staff member. That is not only unfair, it can be debilitating to their heart for ministry.

Empower your kids with a plan for dealing with troubling, difficult, or just nosey people. Even though they are annoying, simply say something like, *"Don't worry, God loves* (Insert name)*, and she needs God to do a work in her heart. We all have things God is working on. Hopefully, she will grow out of her ways one day soon."*

Then run to God and quickly pour out any anger and frustration before you do or say something stupid! Don't fall victim to the "mama bear" reaction here, either. Remember that while she may protect her cubs, mama bear can also do a lot of unnecessary damage to others in the process. Though I know God has given me a great instinct to protect my kids, I must choose to maintain a heart that is not controlled by my flesh, but by His Spirit. Otherwise, it may prove embarrassing later. Ask God to help you know when and how to say the hard things to people, but don't make the mistake of doing it in anger.

If people persist in bothering your kids, I think it is appropriate to set the boundaries yourself. Teach your people that good parents set healthy boundaries when a child needs that. Some people have no filter or social skills, and need *blunt, kind, blunt, gentle, and blunt* boundaries laid out for them. During the difficult season of adoption, well-meaning—but clueless—people tried to help my out-of-control child in ways that were not helpful. We were forced to speak very directly to people and set healthy boundaries for everyone, which wasn't easy. Looking back, I see how God used these situations to help me overcome the need to always please people. I'll elaborate more on this in a later chapter.

Raising a servant

Equally important to protecting our kids from church people is protecting your congregation from your kids. Sometimes ministry can create a monster that your congregation needs to be protected from. Yes, I said a monster. Our children come into the world with a very self-centered, sin nature. If they are catered to and pampered constantly, you may find you have a problem.

A danger in ministry is setting our kids up as prima donnas who use ministry to be the center of the universe. The fishbowl can flatter. Unfortunately, it can also skew reality because it is a small fishbowl. When they step outside the bowl, life will give them a good dose of reality. We can also create an expectation in our kids that ministry is all about the stage. In our celebrity-focused culture, the stage can be a great temptation to an attention-seeking child. We must ask ourselves often as parents: *are we raising servants?* Do we teach our kids that ministry is first, and foremost, about loving God by serving others? Or do they catch a vibe from us that it is about the spotlight? I think the world has enough self-seeking, attention-hungry ministers. I refuse to believe that our kids should be part of that.

Give your kids opportunities to serve. Start with nursery, the bathrooms, and maybe the church kitchen. Have them greet people at the doors of the church, or work alongside and help your custodian. We happen to be blessed with the best church custodian in the world, Mr. Dan, and all of our kids have loved working with him.

Before our kids could teach or perform on a stage, they had to serve in other obscure areas. There have been many great stories and laughter in the car on the way home from church about the not-so-glorious moments of nursery or children's ministry. Each time, we respond: *"You stored up great treasure in heaven today!"* They would roll their eyes, but I think they felt rather good about serving those days because they felt the power of being a team in ministry.

As you and I know, there are many not-so-glorious moments in pastoring, as well. The attitude of a servant is learned best by example. As pastors, we should let God examine our own hearts periodically to make sure *we* have our priorities straight; our kids will usually follow in our footsteps.

Making Your Kids a Priority

Finally, make sure that your kids know they are a higher priority to you than ministry. Schedule special family times that keep everyone connected. Make it a priority to be at their social events, at all costs.

The importance of this was brought home to us during a difficult season when one of our kids was struggling spiritually and making poor choices. Our hearts were broken and we were really concerned that the enemy was embedding a stronghold in our child's life.

My husband and I sat down and told that child that we would do whatever was necessary to help them find freedom. This included walking away from the ministry, if it was necessary, to make that happen. I remember the look on that particular child's face when we said those words. There were no words; just that look of great surprise. And we meant it. Our kids mean that much to us.

You see, if we fail to minister well to the needs of our own kids, I believe we have failed our church congregation. The church needs desperately to know how fathers and mothers should lead and nurture during the difficult times of life. Where should they go, but to those called to lead them? I think that if you have to sacrifice your child for your ministry, you've made a bad trade and done a disservice to both your children and your congregation.

Our responsibility after God, and after our spouse, is to our family. Protect your time together and make sure they have an open door to you always, even during difficult and busy seasons. It is okay to miss a church event to spend time with your kids. Again, the health of your family indirectly impacts your congregation much more than being at every church function. Make your kids a priority and tell them often you are available to them!

A Final Word on Our Children

Finally, there may be a few deeper questions that surface from hurting pastors and pastor's wives. *"How do I deal with parenting failure?" "What if my child is a prodigal? Am I now disqualified from ministry?"* Though it can be tough to minister during painful seasons (see the next chapter), it is important to keep an eternal perspective during these times.

I really don't even like to use those words *"parenting failure"* in the question because it implies that it is the parents' fault whenever a kid rebels and walks away from their faith. I remember often that God is the perfect parent, and He has plenty of prodigals! Why? Because He chooses a relationship of love and gives them the power of choice. Eventually, we, too, out of love must give our children the power to choose. Love must risk hurt by allowing a choice.

I don't believe that our children's rebellion should automatically disqualify us from leadership. I think that gives our kids too much power over our lives and God too little. It is God who calls, qualifies, and empowers us to lead both our family, and our ministry. When your kids reach an age where they have to choose for themselves, their spiritual life must become their responsibility.

Remember, also, that the book of your child's story isn't finished. Just like us, our kids are works in progress as they journey along. I am living proof that just because a child rebels, doesn't mean they will forever live apart from Christ. It was a bad couple of chapters in my story, but my parents didn't write me off as a forever failure. I don't believe God sees our children's rebellion as final, so neither should we. This chapter in their life may be a difficult time of pain and poor choices with which they will have to live, but it is just a chapter.

Nevertheless, authenticity is important. Don't gloss over it by pretending. Just as your kids need to see you grieve over your congregation, your congregation should be allowed to see you grieve over your kids. Both of them are following you somewhere. Let them follow you down the road to grace and healing during the difficult seasons of our lives. Help them understand that though you may suffer in this life, there is a God who cares for you during the process. I think it's also important to be real with your congregation about your mistakes, and the reality that you ultimately have to allow your kids, just like your congregation, to choose whether they will serve Christ.

I have served God long enough now to see how wonderfully able He is, to take that season meant to disqualify us (by our enemy) in ministry, and turn it into something beautiful and useful for service. Remember, God loves redeeming us and bringing glory to His Kingdom in the processes of our lives. Believe that God can do that in the lives of your kids, and what looks like impossibility will begin to look like possibility.

Chapter 8

Help! How Do I Handle Women?

One of the first things I realized when I decided to marry my husband and step into ministry life was that I was different.

First, I didn't know how to play the piano. Fortunately, my mother did. She happened to be at our first youth church plant and I am not sure I would have emotionally survived if she hadn't been there.

Secondly, I wasn't all that quiet or meek. In fact, my husband is being very gracious when he calls me "spirited." That is guy-speak for stubborn.

And third, I, truthfully, struggled to like women. Yes, I admit it.

How was I ever going to be a good pastor's wife? Do you know what I mean about feeling out of place immediately? I suppose some girls don't struggle with this but I certainly dealt with multiple insecurities about my role right from the beginning! I was comfortable in the business world but the church world was scary. I instantly felt like I would never measure up. For women, this can be a real issue.

Unfortunately, there were very few mentors in those early ministry days available to help me learn to navigate these challenges. My pastor's wife was kind, but very busy with her own life and family. She did not seem to have that extra time, nor did I. The only other person I reached out to was caught up in her own insecurities and refused to open herself up, so I was on my own.

Today, we are very blessed to have the technology available to stay connected to people we meet who don't live in our town or go to our church. This is such a blessing, because the connections of mentorship and friendship are available—if we are intentional.

However, we need to learn connect to other women intentionally, inside *and* outside our church. For some of us, this can be very scary and new territory.

Stepping Out of Your Comfort Zone

As I mentioned in the previous chapter, when God adopts us into His family, we gain a perfect Father. He gives us the rights of being a legitimate daughter and invites us to take our place in His family.

Before my husband and I adopted two of our children, A.J. and Mikayla, we sat down with our other kids, Cal and Madison, to get their opinion about the adoption. We wanted to make sure that they were in agreement and supportive of this huge decision. It mattered to us what they thought.

Don't you wish God would ask us what we think about adopting some of our spiritual siblings into His family? To be honest, I sometimes wonder what He is thinking about some of the people He brings into the family of God. But God knows better than to give us that power.

It is easy to forget the depths of the pit God pulled me out of when I come face-to-face with imperfections in someone else. It is easy to overlook things we are capable of, yet hold our neighbor to a different standard. So He doesn't leave it up to us. *He doesn't even ask us what we think!*

While He is perfect, our siblings in Christ, unfortunately, don't have the same standard of perfection. When they come to Christ, they are just like we were: insecure and wounded. They get attitudes. They get scared. They are sometimes fearful of relationships. And when they perceive rejection, they may fight and get nasty.

God asks us to love these people, to overlook their imperfections, to *consider them better than ourselves.* (Philippians 2:3) Despite the difficulty, Jesus says that after loving God above all else, we need to love His people. Somehow, God likes the idea of taking this broken, dysfunctional family, and uniting them into a beautiful picture of His grace. I think He likes to demonstrate His power to transform what seems impossible into great possibilities. There is no other plausible explanation as to how it can happen apart from His power and grace. As ministers of His grace, we must be about the business of building and uniting His family no matter the difficulty.

Whether we like it or not, we also have to face the reality that as the pastor's wife, we have some responsibility towards the women in our congregation. We may not be the designated women's ministry leader. We may not ever lead a Bible study. However, we are looked to as an example of how a woman should live for Jesus, and how we should relate to and love each other as women. And this can be very uncomfortable at times! Many women still battle those wounds and insecurities that started in middle school and they look to us for help. It can create a great deal of tension and pressure in our own hearts if we haven't dealt with our insecurities as it relates to our sisters in Christ. But remember, God chose you because He believes in your ability to rise up through His transforming power and be a beautiful leader for your ladies; you are the leader they need for this time. He doesn't make mistakes; He is making a masterpiece.

Looking back, I am ashamed that there was a time when I dug my heels in the dirt and told the Lord, *"I do NOT like women!"* Sad to say, it's true. Women have a reputation for being catty, superficial, and high maintenance, and I prefer to live in a drama-free world.

Growing up, I found it much easier to play with or hang out with boys. Boys were easy. You always knew where you stood with them; just punch them and find out quickly! With girls, it was not so easy. The rules changed often. Sometimes I wondered whether there were any rules at all!

I understand that not every woman is like this, but it only took a few girls from middle-school to make me gun-shy. So much so, that I walked away from any interest or desire to participate in women's ministries. In those days, I didn't like crafts, baking, or anything remotely related to hospitality. Those things just didn't come easy for me. Unfortunately, those were the stereotypical roles of women's ministries when I was growing up. So I steered clear of this safely for many years.

When I became a pastor's wife, I quietly resisted assuming active roles of ministry to our ladies, except to lead by example or do an occasional small group. But God had a different idea. Doesn't He always? It's strange because I grew up with a sister who was my best friend but here I was, a poser, pretending I liked women, but really refusing to put myself out there or seek developing relationships with any of them. So what was my problem?

A Troubling Pattern

I think the problem stems from this disturbing trend: *we have lost sight of the value of being in a sisterhood.* Society, under the auspice of feminism, has created a culture of competition and division. We have thrown the baby out with the bath water and opted for the Mommy Wars instead. The beauty of our femininity was rejected for a cut-throat mentality to make us be instead more like men. (Not that all men are cut-throat, but I think you understand my point.)

Women are being told to be powerful and strong like men. My question is why can't women just be powerful and strong like a *woman*? Why is strength and confidence seen as a manly trait only?

Further, in whom should we have strength or confidence? The answer, we are told, is we need to have strength and confidence in ourselves. We don't need or want anyone else to have power over us. Unfortunately, we have let life and pain, as a result make us fearful, jealous, shallow, and judgmental of each other. Our girls are growing up striving to impress or outdo each other.

Not sure? Walk into any middle school and observe for more than a few minutes how our girls are interacting with each other. I am concerned with the level of cruelty girls inflict upon each other. It has become survival of the fittest, and some girls are not emotionally surviving the cut. They are coming out hard and cynical. What used to be available in the form of feminine circles to offer us support, encouragement, and guidance has now become groups of antagonistic and competitive women battling each other to be on top.

What we didn't realize was that there was already a God-given power and strength in our femininity designed to be poured out upon the world to make it strong *and* beautiful. Rather than uncover it, we've thrown on the heavy masculine mask of power and called it good. We have lost sight of the benefits and power of being united on the same team with our sisters.

Even within the church—especially within the church—we are suffocating under the pressure to compete and impress each other rather than support and encourage each other. If you want to get strange looks from a woman, ask her what her husband thinks about her new hair style. Her look will usually speak volumes: *"I don't know, I didn't ask."* or worse, *"Why do I care what he thinks?"* It feels like we are striving more to feel beautiful to other women, than for ourselves or our spouse. Somehow that feels rather creepy and twisted. Why does it matter so greatly what other women think of us?

Maybe We Can Find a Better Way?

Proverbs 17:17 says, *"A friend loves at all times, and a brother (or in our case, a sister) is born for adversity."* We were meant to be in relationship, not only with God, but with each other. Sisters were made to live life together, to be there for each other during the difficult times.

Why wouldn't everyone want to live with that kind of relationship? We weren't made to run over each other when we are broken, or mock our sisters when life has hurt them.

During a recent study on sisterhood, the ladies of my church helped me brainstorm some of the real benefits of having a physical sister that we, too often, overlook. The following list is what they came up with.

Sisters:

- *Are fiercely loyal to each other*
- *Yell at each other, but can still hug later*
- *Know each other deeply and love each other anyway*
- *Are forgiving and want the best for each other*
- *Are willing to be vulnerable around each other.*
- *Don't pretend in front of each other. A sister has seen the good, bad, and ugly.*
- *Confront when necessary, unafraid to say the hard things.*
- *Call each other names, but if someone else calls a sister that name—watch out!*
- *Are connected together by love for their parents*
- *Can put aside their issues for those parents*
- *Will move heaven and earth to find a sister in danger.*
- *Laugh, cry, talk, and share secrets late into the night.*

Now I recognize that even biological sisters don't always have perfect relationships that reflect all of these, but I think we can agree that most of the time having a sister can be pretty special.

More than friends, sisters were meant to be there throughout all stages of our life, and when things are tough, my sister is the person I want to be around. I believe that this is the heart of God for His daughters too. United, different, supportive, protective, connected, authentic. Not competitive, divisive, belittling, or envious.

Eventually God began to work on my heart with these truths and really forced me into a corner on this issue. It was frightening because I had to work through so many insecurities that I had with women.

For example, I had no problem speaking in front of an entire congregation with both men and women, but speaking in front of 20-30 women terrified me. Each time I taught or spoke to them, I agonized and prayed through my fear of rejection. Both God and the ladies of my church were gracious. They stuck by me, even when I struggled with what I now consider awful (or at least, awkward) teachings and my discomfort. Most of them were probably oblivious to my internal battles and insecurities.

Soon something began to shift inside of me. I can't even connect it to one particular moment. But somehow, while traveling on this road of obedience, I suddenly found myself surrounded by a team of women that I felt safe with; women that I desired to be around; women with whom I could share ideas and dreams.

In reality, all of these relationships were still subject to all the past issues I had experienced before: *misunderstanding, disagreement, betrayal, etc.* But it was different now. It felt like I was having an epiphany of sorts. The benefit of having close relationships was worth the risks. Maybe you already knew this. I didn't. The ability to call on a group of women who were like-minded (but still diverse) and trust in them to lift me up to God during a storm was impacting me. The joy of laughing together over our uniqueness and crying together over our similar female struggles was something that drew us together, instead of tearing us apart. I realized that if I could have this, so could all of the ladies in our congregation. In fact, to do otherwise would be missing out on something really amazing.

For the past few years now, I've embarked upon an adventure with God and our ladies at Living Hope of building a real sisterhood. It has been a wonderful and frightening process that has brought great benefits to me personally as I've realized the joys of having spiritual sisters.

At times it is scary because we realize the risks of rejection, jealousy, betrayal, or disappointment. However, we are discovering that when a woman knows her true identity in Christ, she is free to take those risks. So we spend an awful lot of time making sure she understands the truth of her identity. We've invested many hours teaching our young girls these truths as well.

This is a very important topic to cover in the discipleship process for women. It helps them to understand that if they get wounded, Christ can heal their wound. If they are rejected for some reason, they remind themselves that Christ always accepts them. Jealousy is not such an attractive option, when they understand that God has a destiny unique for them, one that no one else can fulfill. Yes, God has enough work to go around! And any disappointment in the relationship will only draw them closer to Christ for His care.

I believe these truths will make us a problem–a danger–to the kingdom of darkness. Our sisterhood should be comprised of dangerous women! I think that is what God desires. Women who stand on this solid foundation (*a realized identity in Christ*) will find it easier to love–and live–dangerously. Dangerously vulnerable so that Christ can work not only in us, but through us.

I believe it is time for His daughters, for the sake of their Father, to put aside pretending or holding back relationally in fear for the greater cause: *advancing God's Kingdom and presenting Jesus to people.* Do we have enough faith to believe God will allow us to partake in the wonderful benefits that come as we build our own group of sisters wherever He has placed us?

Remember, it is no mistake. Your women aren't much different than my women. All of them are in need of the grace of God to grow up in Him. All of them were given a beautiful potential that simply needs to be realized. Will you help them see it? I know when we do, we will witness the transforming power of Christ as insecurities, jealousies, and bitter pasts fall away and a cocoon of real beauty and connection begins to open up.

Raising Up a Real Sisterhood

What qualities should our local sisterhoods reflect? I believe the following characteristics are a good foundation on which you can build:

Be open to outsiders. There is safety in belonging. When children belong to a family, they can heal and grow. What was once stunted or immature can be transformed with acceptance and love. This is also true in the Body of Christ. We must recognize the value of each woman who walks into our church. No matter her baggage.

No matter her exterior defensiveness. We need to open ourselves up to accepting them just as they are. Jesus will do the transforming—if we are willing to provide the place where they can heal and grow.

In an adoption, things go much smoother if the new member is readily accepted by the family. That may seem obvious, but it takes real work to integrate new children into a tight family circle. Speaking from experience, it is no easy task.

One of the things we did when we adopted was purposely create *new* family fun traditions. This created excitement in our family that we were able to build on each year so that our adopted children and our biological children could experience these new traditions *together*.

Likewise, within the church, it will take sacrifice and creativity to allow new daughters into our family circle. We, too, will need to continually create an environment that is open to new, bonding ideas everyone can do *together* as we grow the women in our local church. It will take time and positive trust for a new sister to feel safe and loved in our families. Give her that gift and watch the miracle of Christ transform her.

Live committed to each other. Sisters need to be loyal and work together to protect each other. Rather than shunning our sister when she sins, we must learn to be willing to rescue. Not enable, but rescue.

Sometimes we must be willing to gently say the hard words of truth. When we learn to cover (*by refusing to gossip, belittle, or sarcastically tear down)* the value and dignity of each member, we will value the group as a whole. Commit to do life together. Eat together, play together, serve together, and pray together as often as life allows. Make this the culture of your sisterhood. You will reap so many benefits.

Live authentically in your relationships. Sisters must take off the masks and be real. We must stop pretending to have it all together. No one really believes that anyway.

One of the reasons I enjoy taking women out to ride horses is because there are no masks in the barn. It is impossible to pretend to be anything but real when you scoop poop, groom a 1000 lb. creature caked in dirt, or ride across the arena on that same very large and powerful horse. It forces us to be vulnerable and real. The dirt and smells aside, the shining eyes and smiling faces of joy on the face of most women or girls speak volumes. It is here in this environment that the real heart work can begin.

Authenticity does the same thing. When the pressure to perform or outdo one another is taken away, it gives people the freedom to be themselves. It allows Jesus to tear away the pretending and reveal where real healing needs to take place. Confession and truth bring healing. Grow and encourage authenticity liberally in your church and among the ladies you are lucky to do life alongside.

Fill the house with grace-givers. Just as our Father has offered grace to us, so we should offer grace to those around us. Some sisters will be immature, some a bit (or even a lot) rough around the edges, but loving sisters can apply a positive peer pressure for graceful growth in Jesus Christ. We can walk together on the journey of sanctification, encouraging each other to become more like Christ. Admitting our failures and victories goes a long way in providing each other with the faith to keep going when the going gets tough. Iron sharpens iron.

I realize there is no perfect world when it comes to ministering and loving the women in your church. You will have catty, defensive, or even downright mean women walk into your church. Perhaps they were already there when you arrived!

The point is to cast a vision for something greater. Some will stay and be transformed. Others will leave when they become uncomfortable with the change required to get close and sharpen each other.

As the pastor's wife, rather than run out on the idea of a true sisterhood, let's be committed to a better way. God has called you to do your part *(and He will always do His)* to make your place of worship a home for sisters who want to do it differently. Maybe we can positively impact this world together. Maybe Jesus living in us can really be free to make us all different together. And just maybe, the benefits of the sisterhood can outweigh the problems.

The many sisters I have gained through this journey have made the risk and yes, even occasional rejection, worth it. We were born to be daughters of the King. But He also made us to be in a family. While we have many friends, sisters—*real* sisters—are something very special.

You have a wonderful opportunity at your fingertips. Let God's love and grace carry you away from your fears as you step out to dangerously love the women He has put in front of you. Push aside the intimidations or past hurts to allow God to do something amazing in and through you! He will never run out on you, not ever.

Chapter 9

Help! Where Do I Hide in This Fishbowl?

After more than twenty years in ministry, I have discovered one of the most important keys to fruitfulness in ministry. It may surprise you; it may not. Most people think ministry is about a stage, or church growth and numbers. While growth is important, I believe there is something so much greater.

It is about authentically living out your faith in front of others and leading them to do the same. It is a process of making disciples, not just gaining converts. It's about people; the souls of those people are the only thing that last forever.

Keeping First Things First

Oswald Chambers writes in his book, *My Utmost for His Highest*, that salvation is God's work of grace. We sometimes want to take most of the credit in ministry for the awakening process. Yet, the reality is that no one comes to Jesus except the Holy Spirit of God draws that person. Yes, we proclaim the truth of the gospel, but He awakens them and brings them to us.

After proclaiming the gospel, our task is then to make disciples around the world. It is really about duplication. Like Paul, we live it and duplicate ourselves as disciples of Jesus Christ. God has called us as shepherds to lead, protect, and care for His sheep.

As Paul was saying his final farewells to his leaders in Ephesus in Acts 20:28, he commissioned them with this task:

"Keep watch over yourselves and all the flock of which the Holy Spirit has made you overseers. Be shepherds of the church of God, which he bought with his own blood.

We should take this responsibility seriously. Do we value this role and guard carefully our responsibility as shepherds? I hope so. I confess that I don't always feel this way.

Sometimes when you start out in ministry, you are clueless because you are trying to keep your head above the water! My husband and I felt especially helpless during those early years, but we see God was graceful to protect His church until He could help us learn a few things.

Sometimes when you've been in ministry a long time, you can even become hardened to your particular congregation of sheep. Thankfully, God loves our sheep more than we do, so His grace protects them from our mess-ups or difficult seasons of pastoring.

In order to lead sheep, the sheep must be able to see you. If you've ever hung around the sheep pen, you've discovered that you usually wind up smelling like the sheep.

Likewise, the shepherd should smell like the sheep. They must have access to us if we are going to lead them. How can they follow us, if they can't see us? Now for most of us, this can be terrifying! *What if they see my imperfections? What if I stumble along the way?* They will see your imperfections. You will stumble along the way. It's a sign you are a part of the human family. But I have learned that our willingness to be real with people about our struggles and stumbles allows them to see how an imperfect person can and should live out their faith.

Too many leaders in the past have been aloof as the "untouchable ones" and people couldn't relate; or worse, they believed that only a few chosen few could be expected to live a life of faith-filled passion and fruit for Christ. They have fallen victim to the lie that the life of Christ *in* us was somehow out of their reach and meant only for the ministers. What a discouragement that must be to people. Our message as ministers is that the sheep can and should live out their faith by the power of His Spirit and make known the gospel to this world. It is not the job of a select few, but for all of us.

When Troubles Come

But what do you do during the difficult seasons of your life? What about when pain or hard times come, as they always do? How much do you let people in to those times when you are in ministry? How do you walk through this when your whole life is on display and open to judgment and criticism from the entire congregation? Good questions, with no simple answers. Please allow me to give you some helpful tips within a personal story for you.

As I've mentioned, my husband and I started ministry as newlyweds. We went on to have two kids, Cal and Madison, before we were called into the role of lead pastors. In our hearts, we had always thought about having more children through adoption. I think it was a combination of God speaking to us about the needs of lonely kids, and the reality of the pain of childbirth. At any rate, I was not compelled to physically have more children. It had been a very difficult experience and I was sure that there was an easier way. I was both right and wrong. While it may have been easier physically, adoption was a much greater emotional labor of love.

We pursued adoption, and foster parent licensing was the first step. Before his adoption, our son, A.J., had attended our church with his birth father. We spent a great deal of energy helping his dad get on his feet and supporting him as a parent. Unfortunately, things went bad and A.J. ended up under the supervision of the Department of Human Services. Since we were not licensed foster parents yet, he spent some of the early days in a relative placement, and eventually, transitioned into a traditional foster home.

Because of the complications of a personal relationship with his birth family, we chose to stay out of the picture during the reunification period of A.J.'s foster care placement. We made known our willingness to parent, should all other resources (relatives) be exhausted.

The unfortunate part of this is that it takes a *long* time. A.J. spent over a year and half in foster care while we all waited. While he stayed in the same home, he was up and down emotionally with birth parents, and other relatives, in and out of his life during this time. As reunification became less and less of an option for A.J., we faced another surprise twist. A.J.'s birth father had fathered another child during this time, and our daughter, Mikayla, was born into the foster care system. Because the goal was eventually that A.J. would transition into our home, they called us right away so she wouldn't have to be moved again when he was placed in our home.

Sometimes Our Box is Too Small

When we received the call to parent Mikayla, I had been going through a very long waiting season. All of us go through those difficult times in life where God just does not seem to be making any sense.

Have you been there? You think you know what He has in mind and He throws you a curve ball? Maybe, like me, you don't like curve balls. I'm a highly structured person who must have a plan for everything. Suddenly, I was discouraged because every plan I had made came to a screeching halt and I couldn't understand why. What was so perfectly clear to me was, obviously, not so clear to God.

Can I tell you how important it is to trust God during those waiting times? I wish I had been graceful in waiting, but it was not always pretty. There were many crying and whining sessions before the Lord. I doubted my significance. I doubted my purpose. Perhaps in a way, I even doubted His love. All because He had said, "*no*" to several things I had decided I should do.

In hindsight, I realize how small my plans were. This is typically the case. His plans are so much loftier and eternally-focused than our small-minded ideas. So many times, we try to put God into our own little box and ask Him to fit inside of it. He, then, makes a mission out of blowing our boxes apart until we stop imposing our limits and boxes on Him and the plans He has for us. He is looking for us to be daughters who are willing to let go of our ideas and just trust Him without reserve. Our commitment is to Him, not to our personal agenda and what He can do for us. This was, and is still, a hard lesson to learn.

After receiving that phone call to take Mikayla into our home as a foster child, I wept. He had seen the longing in my mother heart. During the foster parent license process, I had felt that old familiar pang for a baby. Now as you might know, healthy infants in foster care are few and far between so the chances were small that I would ever have received a baby. And so I had shared this secret hope with no one, not even Carey. Plus, we were waiting to adopt an older child. But God is the Grand Weaver and is beautifully working even when we can't see it! I realized God knew more than I did about what I needed.

My husband and I readily accepted the role of foster parents and Mikayla came to our home 5 weeks later. She was a beautiful, healthy, baby girl, filled with joy. From the moment she came, she brought our family a great amount of laughter and joy. That has not changed in almost eleven years. We still are amazed how her joy and exuberance has brightened our home and taught us to enjoy life. The unexpected surprises from God's hand are always the sweetest.

After five months of bonding (for which I am very thankful) with Mikayla, plans were made to bring A.J. into our home for permanency placement. The circumstances surrounding A.J.'s placement were much different than those of Mikayla. He had suffered a great loss. Not just once, but multiple times and now—after a year and half in a foster home—he was being moved again. While I knew it would be a challenge, I had no idea what we were getting into.

By the time he came to live with us, A.J. was on six different medications for his out-of-control behavior. He took a pill to help him focus, help him sleep, help him manage his anger (*which didn't work*), help him be happy (*he wasn't*), and the other two were to deal with the side effects of all the rest. In the foster care system, there are levels of "difficulty of care." A.J. was labeled a level three which, at that time, was the highest level. This should have been a red flag to us. But we were confident in our parenting abilities, and this was a child I was going to fix. How hard could it be?

As you can guess, everything went bad pretty quickly. If you don't know anything about children with reactive attachment disorder (RAD), you need to know that they resist and battle those who are closest to them. Suddenly, we were the target of all his rage, anger, and pain. Those battles started immediately and escalated quickly. From the first pencil being thrown across the room to the lawn furniture being thrown across the deck—I knew I was in over my head. This was all in just the *first* week.

Another difficult challenge with RAD children is that worst behavior is reserved for the mother-figure in the home. This means the child acts superficially sweet and charming around others, but focuses the brunt of his anger and rage towards mom.

I began to feel as though I was losing my mind as I battled with him, day after day. My dreams of being his savior quickly disappeared and my goal became that of survival. As his anger surfaced and boiled over, my anger also began to grow. I was angry at this child who had turned my home upside down and was destroying our family joy and peace. I was angry with my husband for thinking he was better than I was at parenting *(A.J. charmed him for quite a while)*. But most of all, I was angry at God for asking me to do something that appeared to be ruining our lives. As I look back now, I am amazed at how God carried us all through that time because I honestly was unaware of His grace as we battled to heal our son, our home, and I, personally, battled my angry heart.

Finding a New Normal

Despite the trouble, God was still looking out for us. He doesn't allow these times in our lives to destroy us, but if we let Him, He hopes to refine and shape us. We say that so often to people throughout ministry, but the true test of faith is when it comes to us personally.

The difficulty of going through this while in ministry is finding that safe place where you can be real, and finding a healthy support system that can hold you accountable. It's hard to get that from the people you are called to shepherd, but God is creative. He will bring people into your life in such creative ways.

During this season, our church was suddenly inundated with several foster and adoptive families. As others heard our story of adoption, God drew other adoptive families that also were living this kind of life to our church. This is a very tight knit community and suddenly, I had a support system of other parents who had children acting out in all kinds of bizarre ways.

It was like a breath of fresh air to my angry heart. I find that God knows exactly what we need during difficult times. So we made a choice to connect these families together and support each other. At one time, we had over thirty-five special needs children in our children's ministry program. Those were difficult days of children's ministry! I formed a small group called *"Special Needs Moms,"* and we got through some very difficult times together and formed deep friendships that have lasted to this day.

Even most of our extended family couldn't understand our struggles, so it was a blessing to be with people who understood. Obviously, I was still the pastor's wife, but I was real in my struggles of adoption. The common struggle of all these families reassured me that I was not losing my mind. My son had deep issues that needed healing. But now I was suddenly in need of emotional healing as well.

I think the greatest suggestion I could give to people who are struggling is to reach out and take a risk. You may be rejected, or you may be overlooked; but it's more likely you may find the comfort of a sister, the arms of a mother, or a friend who can encourage you. Even pastors need people with skin on. We hurt, we bleed, and we need help carrying our burdens. To ignore this need leaves us vulnerable to hardening and bitterness. Look outside of your church. Look outside of your circle. Research and find a place where godly people reside who can carry and support you during those difficult times.

While I wish I could say our son was healed instantly, this didn't happen. Over and over in my private prayer closet, I asked God to take him away and have someone else be his mother. Maybe *begged* is a better word. I didn't want to do this anymore. It was too much.

God knew, though, that not only did A.J. need us in his life, I needed A.J. in my life. He had brought something into the story to ensure I would not quit. It was that joy-filled, baby girl whom I fell in love with almost immediately. It may shock you that I admit this. But I believe God does *nothing* by accident and He knew that my heart would need an anchor to survive the character struggle that would happen during this season. If we gave up parenting A.J., we would have to give up Mikayla, as well. So, my mother heart dug in because that was not an option.

You may feel like judging me for admitting that. I understand. I would probably have thought the same thing had I not lived out the difficulty of raising a child with attachment issues. My other RAD mom friends have felt like giving up so many times and they, too, understood what I was going through. But my husband and I knew that God had called us to this. We weren't sure why He thought we would make a difference as every day felt like failure to us.

Eventually, A.J. began to act out as much for my husband as he did for me. This helped because the honeymoon was over for my husband and we were finally on the same page.

Our research on RAD led us to implement new parenting strategies, called therapeutic parenting, that were unique to kids with attachment issues, to help reign in some of the out-of-control behavior. It required dealing with the ugly behavior when and wherever it occurred.

As A.J. battled to be in control, he reserved his most crafty power plays for public—especially when we were at church—and both of us were always distracted. I can't stress to you the importance of being united with your spouse during difficult seasons. I know I would have never made it through this season unscathed without my husband's support and our unified front. We forced ourselves to implement our strategy of therapeutic parenting, *even* in public. Thus, began one of the biggest spiritual battles of my life.

Giving God Freedom to Prune

Something that I had dealt with for a long time especially since those early days of Bible Quiz came to the surface and God decided to use these circumstances to work it out of my life. I had cultivated a craving for the approval of people.

Most of us have this to some extent when we go into ministry. Our compassion and desire to help people usually forces this to come to the surface at some point in our ministry life. My struggle to keep from being a people-pleaser runs deep.

Suddenly, I was forced to disregard what people thought of us and deal with my son's issues in front of anyone. This was both a terrifying and life-changing process. I had to push past the concern over what people thought about me, if we were going to make any progress. If A.J. forced the power play in public, we dealt with it publicly. That might look like sitting in a time-out somewhere; it might mean sitting with mom instead of going to kid's church; it might even mean standing in the corner while mom finished her conversation. While a few people looked down on us for being so hard on him, most people (at least in our church) were highly supportive.

As my "pleaser" heart went into overdrive, though, I found myself desperately trying to explain myself to every person around me. Finally my husband intervened. His words to me: "*You wouldn't yell at a blind man for stepping on your foot. They can't possibly understand what we are dealing with. Stop trying to explain it to people who can't understand.*" I retorted, "*Well, it doesn't mean my foot doesn't hurt!*"

Nevertheless, I knew he was right. As I stopped explaining myself and begging for others to accept or agree with us, I began to find a new and greater peace. Some people can't understand what you are going through. Some people won't have sympathy or care enough to try to understand. Let them go. Also, let go of the need to defend yourself and your situation. Sometimes people will be cruel, but it is usually because they are blind. And you shouldn't yell at a blind man for stepping on your foot.

Finding Freedom in Yielding

For me, freedom really came down to a choice. It was a choice to give up my fear of what people thought about me as a woman, a Christian, pastor's wife, and yes, even as a mom. A.J. was relating as he raged and battled along with me to let go of his own fears and protective defenses that he thought kept him safe.

When others judged us, they were really telling us they could do the job better. Eventually, I realized that was a farce. No one else was volunteering to do my job. There are thousands of children in foster care at any one time in our country so it's obvious many people aren't willing to do something about the needs of kids in foster care. Finally, I said a genuine *"yes"* to God in submission. I came to grips with the reality that I was the mom that A.J. needed. In fact, I was the mom that God had purposely chosen—in spite of our mess—for him. That was the beginning of real change in both of us.

I wish I could tell you that it became easier all at once. It really didn't. But the greatest lesson I've learned throughout this journey is that love is *always* a choice. Every day I dealt with my child's ugly behavior was another day God showed me the power He gives us to choose to do the right thing and walk in obedience despite what we feel. No excuses, no other choice; just obedience. That was all He was asking of me and finally, that had to become my daily goal.

I find it ironic that this was the very thing we were teaching our son. *Stop with the excuses of your pain, your past, your helplessness—it is no longer helping you. Walk in obedience with trust that we love you and are doing what is best for you.* And these daily, small, choices of obedience change us forever.

As I yielded myself in trust over and over to the hands of a loving God, the shackles of people-pleasing began to slowly fall off. Suddenly, I found myself not afraid to speak to the hard things. As a result, even ministry confrontation became less difficult because love is always a choice, even if it's hard. If we love the people we shepherd, we will be willing to say the hard things. Not mean things, just those sometimes, difficult words of courage and love. Words to encourage them to do the hard things and believe that God's power can work in their lives as well, if they are willing to trust God.

My healing from the drive of people-pleasing and my anger towards God seemed to mirror A.J.'s healing. We are not finished even today after many years, but I have realized that God can be trusted and we always have a choice. Even when it feels like He made a mistake.

When you answer the call of God and yield to love in obedience, He is doing something very deep in you. It isn't always pretty, because in spite of His faithfulness, we are sometimes very unfaithful. But this we can know: the difficult seasons of our lives are *opportunities* for God to change us, heal us, and lead us into greater fruitfulness, especially in ministry. We don't get to choose when or how pain comes into our lives, but we can choose to never let it be wasted.

The greatest lesson any of us can learn from difficult seasons is that God specializes in redeeming our pain for His glory. You don't have to hide in the fishbowl. God has called you and your spouse to walk with grace before Him, and before the people you lead, even when life becomes difficult. This is merely the opportunity He is looking for to be glorified through your difficulty.

I pray your lives inspire the faith of those who follow you. Guard your heart from anger. Don't waste great energy defending yourself all the time. Listen to God when He speaks to you.

Finally, realize that freedom to be the woman or man that God wants you to be will come one obedient choice at a time. A life well-lived is lived one obedient choice at a time. The fruit of our obedience is always worth the cost. Do it God's way even when it is difficult, and watch Him produce great fruit internally that will only enhance your ministry externally.

Chapter 10

Help! I Feel Like I'm Falling Apart!

They seemed like the perfect ministry couple. Charismatic, strong, beautiful, and grounded in the Word of God. We all expected to see God do great things through their ministry. So what happened?

When the news of their marital separation and resignation from ministry reached me, my heart sank. Not again. This happens too often in ministry. No one really knows the inside story because in the midst of the chaos, the truth gets muddied and defenses go up.

But one thing we do know is that it leaves all of us—church, ministry partners, friends, and of course, family—reeling in pain in the aftermath. It is a great tragedy because so many people are affected and disappointed by the actions of one couple; unfortunately, some are broken beyond healing. Our service in ministry has such a rippling impact on people and sometimes, it's hard for us to see in the confusion of our own chaos and personal issues.

Carrying the burdens of people takes a toll on your personal life. If self-care, spiritual rest, and family aren't properly prioritized, it won't be hard for the enemy to take down any couple with the pressures and demands of ministry.

Finding A Place of Rest

No matter how long we have been in ministry or how well prepared we are, there will come a day (or several days) when we will need to step back and take a time-out from the pressures of ministry, and simply rest. I cannot stress the importance of this enough.

In addition to implementing boundaries as discussed earlier, pastors and their families must learn to care for themselves and find ways to refresh often from the burdens of ministry or they can easily self-destruct. Too many of us wait until we are emotionally wiped out, or on the verge of a nervous breakdown, before we give ourselves the permission to opt-out and take a breather.

But how do we do this when the pressures and needs of people are continually coming at us? This has been one of my greatest struggles in ministry because the needs never stop. Sometimes I think I've expected Jesus to chase after me so he can throw His grace on me as I quickly pass by in my hurried state. I've expected that rest should come without anything being required of me, and everything given to me. However, this misses out on the true beauty of spiritual rest.

Before you can expect rest, you must make a place for rest. You must make a place where you delegate someone to cover those needs so that you can allow God to refresh you. There is no shame in that. In fact, great men or women recognize their own limitations and protect their church from those weaknesses out of love. If you have no one to delegate those pressing needs to, then take the bold step of declaring a time of rest anyway. I doubt there is little you can offer in the way of help when you are emotionally frazzled and spiritually drained anyway. Your church would be better off without your help in those instances. It may also surprise you how well they find a way to cope or pull together when you are taking a rest.

Believe it or not, making the place for rest in our lives is the easy part. The harder part is truly learning to rest and disconnect. I believe it starts with a proper understanding of this idea of *rest*.

One of my favorite scriptures on this subject is found in Psalm 23. Most of us can quote this chapter by heart. Unfortunately, this scripture is reserved more often for an expository preaching on death, rather than a practical teaching for everyday life. Though I totally understand why it would be shared during a funeral, I encourage you to make it an essential part of your daily life. Let's read it together:

The Lord is my shepherd; I shall not be in want.
He makes me lie down in green pastures,
he leads me beside quiet waters,
he restores my soul.
He guides me in paths of righteousness
For his name's sake.
Even though I walk through
the valley of the shadow of death,

I will fear no evil,
for you are with me;
your rod and your staff,
they comfort me.
You prepare a table before me
in the presence of my enemies.
You anoint my head with oil;
my cup overflows.
Surely goodness and love will
follow me all the days of my life,
and I will dwell in the house of the Lord forever.

Here is a beautiful picture of rest. It is place of solitude, quiet, rest, refreshing (water and food), anointing, and blessing.

If you have spent any time at all around farm animals, you will understand that a pasture equals rest, refreshing, and restoration. In fact, our horses waste no time after the saddles are off their back to run like crazy for the pasture. It is a moment of anticipation and excitement. If you get in their way, you may get run over or kicked in the excitement! They make sure to take a long refreshing drink, and many love rolling around in the dirt or grass. Within minutes, they are replenishing on either grass or the enormous round bale of hay provided for them. After they have worked hard, the pasture is the place they desire to be. In fact, most of them leave that pasture rather reluctantly because it is their "happy" place where everything is good.

What about you? When was the last time you anticipated a time of rest and refreshing? If you are like most of us in ministry, it is a vague memory. Where is your place of rest, refreshing, and restoration? I'm not referring to a physical place, though you may have a place physically where this occurs most often.

All of those things necessary for true rest are found in only one place: *the presence of the Shepherd.* Isaiah 26:3 says, *"You will keep in perfect peace all who trust in you, all whose thoughts are fixed on you!"* (NLT) You can sleep for hours, take a long vacation, even spend the day at the spa, and still not be truly be rested. True spiritual and emotional rest is found in the peace of God's presence.

It is a place where you cast off the cares, worries, and burdens that you have carried into His presence and replace it with peace and healing, followed by the unlimited restoration and refreshment of His grace. It is in this place that all thirst and hunger is quenched. It's the place Jesus spoke of when talking with the woman at the well.

I find it beautiful that after the Psalmist mentions rest, healing, and refreshing, he, then, mentions a great anointing. Too many times, we walk around wounded, angry, or simply exhausted and cannot figure out why there is no fruit in our work, no life in our ministry, or worse, no joy in our hearts! It is the breath of the Shepherd that will revive those dry, dead bones we bring to Him so that there is life again in us and in our ministry service.

Think for just a moment about the reality of life you face in ministry. You deal daily with poverty, sickness, death, divorce, abuse, addiction, chaos, conflict, spiritual brokenness, and probably much more. When I went through the social work program at Ferris State—a very liberal program—they taught us the importance of practicing self-care and finding healthy outlets to help us step away during the difficult seasons and cope with the pressures of OPD (Other People's Drama).

I worry that we aren't teaching (or even giving permission to) our pastors and families to do the same. You are not the savior of people's souls. You are not the Great Physician. If you try to be those things, you will suffer and your family will suffer. Too many times, we rely on our own power to meet the needs of people, or worse, our own self-worth, instead of relying on God's power to help people find their true worth in Christ. You are your church's shepherd. You hope and pray that they will follow you. Jesus is your Great Shepherd. He hopes and prays that you will follow Him when He leads you into the pasture of His presence for an extended time of rest. Too many of us don't and we end up reaping a chaotic whirlwind, as a result.

Resting under the Shepherd's Protection

The kids and I used to raise lambs to show at our local 4-H program every summer. They were some of the dumbest animals we have ever had. They were skittish, scatterbrained, and so frightened of everything.

When transitioned from one place to another, they are also prone to sickness and digestive issues. Their care is very important so they can thrive and gain weight. To the 4-H kid, weight gain means money! The problem arises when it comes time to get your hands on them to care for them. You see, when you first bring them home, they will have nothing to do with you.

One day our lambs were severely sick with diarrhea. Our lamb "mentor" told us to administer Pepto-Bismol to each of them. My first thought was that she was kidding. She was not. My second thought was that she was crazy. She might have been. But she truly expected that we would catch those crazy lambs and somehow get Pepto-Bismol down their throats. In hindsight, it is a miracle that we didn't kill them as we chased them around that lamb pen trying to get pink stuff down their throats! They were so frustrating because they didn't understand that we were only trying to help them as we chased them around and around in exhaustion.

How many times can we respond like that to God when He is trying to help us? Sheep are a beautiful analogy of humanity but not for the reasons you think. Yes, they are dumb, and we can all agree that humans can be, sometimes, very dumb. More importantly, sheep are a great example of an animal created with very little self-protection. They clearly were not created to survive on their own. Their very design precludes them from self-care.

Think about that for a moment. They are lost without the care of a shepherd. They don't have sharp teeth, great strength, quick speed, or much of anything to protect them from their enemies, except maybe an annoying bleat. They are safest and healthiest when cared for by a shepherd. I think sheep are a great picture of the vulnerability of humanity without a God. He needs to protect us from the dangers that lurk in our world. But we run, and run, and run *away* from Him, instead of *to* Him.

David understood this when he wrote Psalm 23. He spent many nights looking after his lambs while they slept. He watched out for them. He kept them safe from the elements and the predators. Whatever happened, he was there to protect his sheep. God desires to protect us, too, from our predator and the natural cares of life so we can grow healthy and strong in Him.

Resting under the Shepherd's Guidance

The Shepherd also provides guidance for the lamb. They need His guidance during the dark or stormy times because they can't always see the path. Two of our lambs, Legolas and Gimli (named after *Lord of the Rings* characters), had a terrible tendency of getting out of their pen and getting lost. Often, our neighbors would call us to tell us that the lambs were loose and running through their yard.

One day, they ventured up onto the neighbor's deck and stood on top of the hot tub staring into the back patio window of their house. It was a moment of great embarrassment. Whenever they were lost, Legolas and Gimli would call out until they heard my daughter's voice. Then they would run through the woods towards the voice they recognized, bleating all the way! It was a beautiful picture of how important it is to know our Shepherd's voice. It brings to life the words of Jesus, when He said, *"...and his sheep follow him because they know his voice."* (John 10:4)

Do you know His voice? When ministry gets frightening, depressing, or just discouraging, have you stopped and listened for His voice through all the other noise? I must confess—too often—I've called my mom, my husband, or my friends before I called out and listened for God's voice when I am struggling. Often, I can find myself in such a confused state because I've let everyone else, *except* Him, into my head.

His peace will come when we hear His voice above all the other distractions. Then we follow Him through the dark parts of the trail, even when the enemy feels so close. He guides us back to the pasture for safety and rest and allows us to drink of the still waters. Maybe He even uses his rod as both a source of comfort during the rainstorm to remind of His presence, or as source of discipline when we are moving off the right path. Lean into that guiding rod no matter how you feel when it touches you. You will always find rest under His guidance.

Resting under the Shepherd's Care

A good shepherd also provides care for his lamb. When the lamb is injured or sick, the shepherd is the one responsible for her care. She is completely dependent on the shepherd for the right remedies and medications while she is sick.

God, our Shepherd, also desires to administer care to us, because we are often wounded, bleeding, sick, or just worn out inside. Sometimes though, it can feel vulnerable to let someone care for us. So many of us don't like feeling vulnerable!

When He touches that scar, we flinch and good ole' self-reliance tries to rear its ugly head again. We jump up and hurry along before the wound has healed. All the while, He is trying to apply sutures to your open wound.

Maybe as a woman, you have received poor care in the past. Perhaps it was at the hands of a father, a lover, a husband, or a brother. Why would you ever want to let anyone care for you again? But God is not your father, your lover, or your brother. He is a *good* Shepherd. Jesus said in John 10:11, *"I am the good shepherd. The good shepherd lays down his life for the sheep."* His heart is one of a good Father who desires to care for you, out of the abundance of His love *if* you will only let Him.

While He cares for His lamb when she is sick, He also cares for her when she is well. If He only cared for her during her sick times, He would be a neglectful Shepherd. But He provides her food for strength, water for refreshing, a safe place to lie down to restore the body and the mind of the lamb.

Just like any wellness plan, prevention is the best approach to staying healthy. If you want to be at your peak spiritual health, you must practice the art of surrender regularly so God can provide you with the refreshment you need. It looks like this: *partaking of His Word in a quiet moment; casting off all those burdens you've carried home; drinking from His well of grace in your prayer time for strength; and following the leading of His voice as you journey.* There are so many more things we miss because we refuse to rest and allow our mind, will, and emotions to be restored to a right perspective by His presence.

Obstacles to Rest

Sometimes the refusal to rest stems from a lack of trust. Do you see that everything you need comes from His hands? Are you afraid that what you need is found elsewhere? When you choose to lie down beside those quiet waters for healing and care, He will feed you from His table, whatever you have need of: compassion, forgiveness, freedom from resentment and bitterness, or any of the ugly things that ministry dredges up during the storms. You must understand this truth if you are going to survive the difficult days.

One of the first lessons I learned when I went into the ministry was that I had major trust issues! Of course, I didn't trust God enough to let Him care for me. I didn't trust people because I feared being kicked around. I struggled to trust my husband because my heart was still wounded and insecure. God desires to do what is necessary to help us, but we must learn to acknowledge, and then set aside, our fears long enough to get close to Him. It's easier to just run in circles, away from Him. So we think—until we become so sick that we can no longer run.

What are your fears? Is it the fear of being rejected, the fear of failure, or just the fear of disappointing people, or even God? If you just keep moving, you can keep juggling everything with your own self-reliance. God desires you to stop and rest. Let go of your fears and get away to His pasture until you safely trust Him again.

Another obstacle to rest is discontent. *What keeps you from being content?* Those words, *"The Lord is my shepherd, I shall not want..."* sometime haunt us because we find that rest will not come when we are consumed with our wants.

You see, discontent leaves a person in a perpetual cycle of frustration. It is hard for our "Madison Avenue" culture to understand what it means to *not* be in want. We spend our lives pursuing material things. Our hearts are rarely satisfied— just one more thing, one more purchase, that's all we need! His sheep have become consumers who want the wrong things.

Jesus must have experienced similar issues with his disciples because He told them: "*...do not worry about your life, what you will eat; or about your body, what you will wear. Life is more than food and the body more than clothes." (Luke 12:22-23)* We can spend all this energy worrying, planning, and buying things for ourselves.

Ultimately, we become enslaved to those very things we thought would fill us. When Jesus said to provide purses for ourselves that don't wear out, He wasn't referring to a Coach or Gucci purse! He was directing our discontented, enslaved hearts to the freedom of the pasture where every need we have can be met by the Good Shepherd as we seek first an eternal kingdom—a treasure that will last forever. There is nothing in this material, finite world that was meant to fill what only God can fill.

I have found over the years that the more I release my wants or desires to Him, the more I have come to enjoy the things that I have. He wants you to enjoy the things right in front of you. This is easier if you can rest knowing God will give you all that you need. I believe it gives Him great joy to have daughters who can look in His face and say, *"The Lord is my shepherd, I shall not want..."* and truly mean it.

Insist on a Sabbath

During the most wearisome times of ministry life, I have found that when I stop running and rest in His presence, He is free to do the necessary work in my heart so that I have the strength to get up and go on.

Since those early days, we have learned to schedule rests for our family. For us, vacations are not merely times of blustery activity. Our kids sometimes grumble because we don't plan huge vacations across the United States very often. In fact, a great part of our vacation is spent simply resting and unwinding. This is *no* easy task in the days of text messaging, social media, and smartphones.

Some of my greatest memories are from those moments in our own backyard sitting around a camp fire just reconnecting and talking to each other. My kids, especially, struggled as they hit the teen years because we are usually wrapped up in our church family life. They used to balk when we went on vacation because it meant they had to go to church somewhere else! While we were thankful they loved their church home so much, we insisted. We insisted because we needed time away for that refreshing so we could better serve our church. Though they couldn't totally relate to the burden we carry, they respected it. They loved our church enough to stop balking.

Insist on some type of Sabbath rest for everyone in your family at least weekly. Then schedule bigger periods of rest during vacation times. It will pay great dividends.

Peter gives great insight for ministry families in 1 Peter 5:2-4:

"Be shepherds of God's flock that is under your care, serving as overseers—not because you must, but because you are willing, as God wants you to be; not greedy for money, but eager to serve; not lording it over those entrusted to you, but being examples to the flock. And when the Chief Shepherd appears, you will receive the crown of glory that will never fade away."

As I've mentioned, we are called to lead those under our care, foremost by our examples. What kind of examples are we to be? I believe we are called to be an example of daughters and sons who enjoy Him every day. Out of that enjoyment, flows our service. We carry the responsibility of being an example of a husband and wife who reflect what two people in love look like. We show them what a healthy marriage looks like. We show them how to lead a home that is committed to following Christ with a clear vision. We teach them what it looks like to raise kids who are fun to be with *(even when they are not fun to be with)* and, hopefully, will eventually follow Jesus, too.

Too many times we divide ministry and family into two separate entities. Your greatest gift in ministry to your congregation is the example (not perfection) that you show them. You show them how to get up and start over when you are hurt. You teach them how to serve in the midst of your pain. You show them how to go to your Shepherd for His care. You show them how to follow your Shepherd as He leads you. You, then, turn to those who follow you and say, *"Follow my example, as I follow the example of Christ."* (1 Cor. 11:1)

Paul and Peter had this figured out as they served in ministry. It was good since they faced great persecution. You need to follow your Shepherd. You need to listen to your Shepherd, especially when He tells you to rest. When He comes close to restore, don't run away.

One last thing that I personally recommend for self-care: find something to do *outside* of the church that refreshes you.

Maybe this surprises you, but I genuinely mean it. You need to get away from the church world from time to time. First, I think pastors and pastor's wives should purposely rub shoulders with unbelievers so we don't become isolated in our Christian bubble and forget how to live in this world without being of this world.

Secondly, just because you are called to ministry doesn't mean you have to be dull and boring. In fact, if you are going to lead by example, you should demonstrate the full and adventurous life of a Spirit-filled believer. Get off your seat and explore the world God created as a wedding gift for you. Jesus was certainly not dull. He didn't always play it safe. He went into the mountains for rest. He went fishing with His friends.

Find something that stirs your passion and helps you refresh and burn off emotional energy, especially as you get older before you become a creepy creature of habit. I pray my kids have to work hard to keep up with Carey and me, as we do life together. Tired and exhilarated children rarely have time for trouble!

Though my husband and I do many things together, I find some of my greatest refreshing comes from being in the barn with my horses. He, unfortunately, doesn't love it. He doesn't quite understand how getting dirty and working with horses can be refreshing. But this is ok! I don't expect that he has to understand it. It is refreshing to my soul. When I am with my horse, I feel God's pleasure.

Where do you experience His pleasure? Maybe it's been awhile since you've felt any pleasure. It's time—for your benefit and those you love—that you practice incorporating healthy physical and spiritual rest in your life. Great anointing, goodness, and mercy will all come when you follow your Shepherd to a pasture of rest, refreshing, and yes, restoration. Let go of your fears and release those "things" that keep you from a contented rest. Unload your burdens unto His capable shoulders and then allow yourself the joy of knowing your Shepherd and enjoying Him forever!

Chapter 11

Help! What if I'm Bleeding Inside?

I wasn't quite sure what was happening, or why it was happening. Here I lay on the bed weeping and trying so hard to explain myself to my husband. He didn't understand what was happening to me, which was a bit frustrating for both of us. For him, it wasn't such a big deal; it was just a bump in the road of ministry, but I felt that my heart had been broken.

As I wept, I complained and bemoaned to him my disbelief that God would let this happen to us when we had been so faithful to Him. Carey kept reminding me over and over that we just needed to do what was right. When you are trying hard to rationalize a poor attitude, those reminders get a little annoying. Finally, I cried out in frustration, *"I'm dying here!"* My husband paused for a moment and then in a very quiet and calm voice answered, *"I think that's the point."*

There was silence in the room and I think he wondered for that brief moment if I wasn't ready to haul off and smack him! But the reality and truth of his words sank deep down into my heart at that moment.

It wasn't that God was merely "letting" this happen. It was that He was trying to work in my life and all I was doing was complaining about it. I began to weep again. But this time it was different. I realized what was happening here, and even though I didn't like it, I knew that it was the voice of the Lord that spoke at that moment through my husband.

Was I willing to lay down all my expectations and rights before the Lord so He could be glorified in my life? Was my flesh going to die so that my spirit could live? I had a choice and that choice determined the effectiveness with which I would serve. Was I willing to lay that anger down and serve someone *again* who had betrayed us in the past, even though I felt it was unfair of God to ask?

As I released my anger through my tears, I felt God's peace wrap around me and hold my broken heart close to His. I was right where I needed to be. I hadn't seen it. I certainly hadn't felt it, but God, in the midst of this pain, was holding my heart carefully and reminding me that He would never run out on me. The choice to keep my heart soft and available to Him, or not, was mine.

The Reality of Ministry

I doubt anyone wakes up in the morning and says, *"I can't wait for someone to hurt me today!"* Inevitably though, it happens. As you will find (or have already found) when you lay down your life and family to serve in ministry, there are many opportunities to be hurt or rejected. But you do have one choice. You always have a choice in how you handle that hurt.

My purpose in this chapter is to walk through some of the practical wisdom we have learned in these difficult situations. You and your spouse may face some of these situations, or completely different ones. Regardless of the difficulty of the situation, how you handle them is the most important thing. Allow God to help you choose the right attitude. What matters most is that you always remain teachable.

This was the greatest lesson we learned through our hardships in ministry. God is always working. Not just in the lives of your members, but also in the refinement of your character. We just need to stop and ask the question, *"What is He teaching me?"* Usually, it is easier (and our first reaction) to assume that the other person is just wrong. Sometimes they are. But sometimes, we are wrong. No matter who is wrong, we know that all the time God is using that person or situation to grow us into stronger and better women and leaders.

Along with remaining teachable, we must also remain humble. If we don't lead from a foundation of humility, we will find ourselves in trouble quickly. If we have a need to always be right, be first, or be affirmed, the ministry lessons will be harder, longer, and unfortunately, more frequent.

So start with this basic idea: *"God opposes the proud but gives grace to the humble."* (James 4:6b) Whatever we do, we will need God. Otherwise, He will use ministry to break us until we come to that conclusion on our own. You will find no shortcut here.

Too often, churches are filled with prideful leaders acting out of their insecurities, rather than a spirit of humility. We need to stop and ask ourselves, *"Why am I doing this anyway?"* If we want to be on God's side, we must always lay aside our pride. It is not about whether God is on my side, or your side, or anyone's side. We must posture ourselves to be on God's side. His side is one of truth, holiness, love, maturity, and always, humility. If we desire His grace, it starts with our humility.

If you intend on finishing ministry well, you will need God's grace for every part of your life. If you love people more than you love being right, God will be able to bring you out of your circumstances more pliable *and* more anointed than you were before. If you insist on the path of pride, you will find Him opposing you at every turn.

Please forgive the repetition, but this was a tough lesson for me. My streak of prideful perfectionism left me highly intolerant for quite a few years, and God has had to break that in me. I hope you learn quickly, or you, too, may find yourself listening to God chuckle when you finally (*and humbly*) come to the realization that He knows more than you do. So let's start with some of the common hurts that pastors and pastor's wives face.

When Someone Leaves Your Church

Your stomach gets a sick feeling way down deep. Your heart races as your emotions begin to soar internally, and you desperately struggle to hide it. Words are noticeably missing, as you stumble over what to say next. You pray inwardly that God gets you out of here quickly, so you can be alone. You need to be alone so that you can deal with whatever is happening on the inside of you.

Does this sound familiar? These are some of the things that happen inside of me whenever I hear news that someone I care about is leaving my church. Obviously, if they aren't really connected, it impacts me less. If they are part of our church family, though, you can count on this being my initial reaction.

Why is this one so hard? While there are times where I wish I didn't care, I realize that when someone leaves my church the wrong way, my feelings are a reflection of what has happened to our relationship. Our relationship has been torn, divorced, shattered, or ripped away.

Notice, I said, *the wrong way*. There is a right way to leave a church. Unfortunately, most people don't know it, or lack the courage to leave the right way. (See my husband's book, *On This Rock*, for more on this.) It is better to tell your pastor that you feel it is time to leave, rather than just leave abruptly out of fear of confrontation. Talking about it with your pastor means caring enough about them and the church to face any fear with courage, rather than risk hurting them.

When people leave the right way, it preserves the relationship and allows for closure which is healthy. Without that closure, there are only assumptions. If you have a vivid imagination (as most of us do), those assumptions are usually negative.

Sometimes years after people have left our church, I will hear bits and pieces of the real story why they left. For years, I just assumed they disliked us, or I assumed that we had offended them in some way. While some did have those issues, more of them were struggling with personal issues. For them, it was just easier to walk away, rather than be vulnerable enough to talk to someone.

Unfortunately, by the time you learn this, you've had many years to formulate a negative conspiracy of why they left. It's hard for most people to understand the emotional energy that pastors and pastor's wives spend on people who leave the church, or what it does to them personally. If they were to leave the right way, much of this could be avoided.

Nevertheless, you don't always have this luxury. So what can you do? When you hear the news of someone leaving from a third party, say very little. I mean this. Say too much, and you may sin! Proverbs 10:14 says, "...the babbling of a fool invites disaster." As your emotions begin soaring, you are liable to say something stupid. Receive the information with a simple, *"Wow, that's too bad."* or *"That makes me sad."*

Also, avoid defending yourself, or worse, jumping into building a case against them. It's not right to begin tearing them apart. I know you may feel like they deserve it, and maybe they do. But others in your church are taking their lead from you, and it reveals an insecure leader when you lash out. Despite your initial anger or hurt, I think it's important to say as little as possible.

After you've received the information, you need to share it with your spouse. However, don't share it with your pastor right before he is getting up to preach unless it is something that could blindside him; in that case, tell him immediately. I recommend you pray together right away for the mind, heart, and peace of Christ to bring order to the storm of chaos that swirls in your brain. You may feel so many different emotions: betrayed, angry, disappointed, or just simply hurt.

Whatever you feel, I recommend you take it to Jesus right away so that no root of bitterness can form. The hard part is that sometimes you have to get through ministry obligations when you are reeling on the inside. I have been through those moments. They are truly moments where you feel you are bleeding on the inside, while everything continues on around you and no one seems to understand.

Here are a few of my suggestions for surviving these first few difficult moments and days:

- **Whisper out to Jesus each moment you feel like you will lose it.** In our weakness, God's grace comes through.

Resist the urge to run away from God. If you are mad at Him, tell Him. But always stay connected. You will need His strength and grace to do what is right through the process.

- **Find a faithful friend who won't ask questions and ask them to pray for you.** I have a couple of those dear friends who don't ask, but will simply put their arms around me and pray whenever I ask. I am so grateful.
- **Keep your schedule light.** You are grieving. You have suffered a relationship loss. I liken people leaving our church to a divorce involving children. You have to be the adult (or in this case, mature spiritual adult) while your children (congregation) grapple with the loss. They may get to maintain connections, while you are often shut out. This is difficult but give yourself permission to grieve this loss and you fill find healing will come quicker than if you sweep it under the rug.
- **Read the Word of God out loud.** Those inner voices in your head are very loud when you feel rejected or betrayed; read, instead, what God says to you and about you in His Word so His voice is louder.
- **Pray for those who have hurt you**. This may feel impossible at first. So pray *whatever* you can muster at that moment. Jesus says to do this, so trust Him. Eventually, if you desire to be whole, you need to forgive them and let them go. Praying to bless them puts you in that place.
- **Establish healthy boundaries**. When my heart is hurt, I may need some space from places where these people frequent. Even viewing their Facebook page may keep you strung along emotionally. Restrict viewing their post (see the help function) in your newsfeed or viewing their page every day. When people are nasty or chucking spears at us, or the church, I have no problem de-friending them altogether. My heart needs to get healthy.

There will be times when your heart will bristle and scrape that crusted scab, and you bleed again. Take it back to Jesus again and again. Keep your own heart pure before Him and He will pour out great grace that will be sufficient to carry you during the weak moments. One day, I promise you, it will be easier. You will move on, and so will your church.

Over the years, we have learned that a church will usually cycle every few years with transition. Not every person will fit your church's personality. You may even be happy, or at least, relieved when a few of them leave. The hardest ones will be those you spent the most time with in friendship or mentoring, or the ones who are just plain nasty about the way they leave.

Again, it isn't about who is right. Sometimes we must just do what is right. God will vindicate us when we are wronged. If you take matters into your own hands, you will mess it up. Be honest about your hurt, but refuse to enter the drama. When you roll in the mud with a pig, you just get yourself dirty; then you realize the pig likes it.

When Someone Speaks Against Your Husband

I am a justice-seeker at heart. I like to think this is why I went into ministry and social work. Unfortunately, it creates difficulty for me from time to time, especially when someone speaks poorly about my husband. These are probably the hardest moments for me because I live with him. He is one of the most giving people I have ever known. He is the real deal, and has given up so much of his life to help others find Christ.

When people say things that bring his character into question, I have a tendency to overreact. Over the years, he has asked me to always direct that person (if they speak something negative to me) back to him. I used to try to defend him, but found myself speaking for him, which is a dangerous thing. People can quickly twist your words and make the situation much worse. So, it is usually better to reply with a simple, *"That doesn't sound at all like my husband, I recommend that the two of you get together immediately to clarify these things. Would you like me to have him call you?"* Avoid triangles, at all costs. A triangle is where people come to you to fix things in another person, usually to avoid dealing directly with that person. This is not fair to you, or to your husband, so avoid the relationship triangles.

When Someone Gossips About You

Occasionally, you may overreact when you are upset. Maybe it will help explain what happened one day when I was dealing with a young lady who struggled with being a gossip. I really can't explain why it happened, but I can tell you it was not planned.

This particular young lady sporadically attended our church, briefly came to us for counseling with her then-husband, and had just gone through a divorce. After a couple of these counseling appointments with my husband and I, she decided to throw my name out there as the one who told her that she was justified in getting a divorce, plus a lot of other incorrect information.

I have a personal policy to refrain from ever telling people they should, or should not, divorce. I am very adamant about this. They alone have to live with the ramifications of a decision of this magnitude, so I make it a practice not to suggest or affirm this to anyone. This may explain my mindset that day.

My husband decided to ask her to come in since she had made the mistake of telling a close friend of mine this information. I was grateful that the friend came to me right away when it didn't sound right to her. I sat next to this gossiping girl, fuming; as I listened to her explain the situation with a superficial civility that was personally grating to listen to.

My husband paused for a moment, trying to find the right words in response, and at that moment, looked over at me. Something came over me. I don't know if it was the Holy Spirit. Whatever happened, it was fueled by a righteous anger and disgust with her pretending spirit. It came out as both a holy rebuke and a confronting of a lying spirit. I like to describe it as a *"verbal spanking"* so we could deal honestly with the character issues that were underneath.

My husband just stared at me in shock. He had never witnessed this before. Neither had I. I haven't done it since. When I finished, I told her that I cared about her, and if there was going to be any restoration, it needed to be founded in truth and she needed to stop sinning.

She stared at me strangely for a moment and then to my surprise, she apologized to me. Maybe she was scared not to, but she truly seemed repentant. After that, everything in our relationship was good. Though she didn't stay at our church (this was no surprise, as she was never a regular attender), we are both to this day very comfortable with each other. There is no awkwardness in our relationship any longer. I certainly don't recommend this approach in every situation. But when you are dealing with a person who is a gossip, or has a lying tongue, you must cut through the tongue-twisting and deceiving that they regularly practice and call it out. Though you should always wrap it in love, directness is certainly called for in the gossip situation. Gently rebuking someone who has a divisive tongue can save a great deal of trouble later.

When the Opposite Sex is Getting Too Close

I think the best defense is a good offense. Every minister and minister's wife should have clear, protective boundaries to prevent anyone getting too close. My husband has done a great job making sure that he minimizes time with members of the opposite sex, especially in counseling situations. This is so important. He has a window in his office door which is connected to the main office. He usually refers women who are in need of ministry to one of our female staff members, or me.

While, I realize some ministers don't have female staff to help out in this area, I highly recommend the pastor look to a spiritually, mature woman in the church to help in this area to avoid the usual bonding that takes place in counseling, especially when dealing with emotionally-charged situations. A minister should not be in a car alone, or go out to lunch alone, with a member of the opposite sex. Paul says we should *"flee the very appearance of evil."*

The boundaries of the minister or the minister's spouse are necessary to protect the minister, spouse, family, the other party, and the church. It leaves the enemy no wiggle room to call into question the character of a pastor. I, especially, caution pastors who work in youth, or music ministry to have very healthy boundaries. It's easy to get caught up in feeling obligated to give a ride home to a teenager; or spending extended time together practicing for events where you can find yourself suddenly alone with a member of the opposite sex.

This works both ways. The pastor's wife also needs to have protective boundaries in place. There seems to be an increase in stories of women reconnecting lately with an old flame or boyfriend on social media. It doesn't take too much contact with someone and suddenly, you find yourself emotionally attracted to someone other than your spouse.

Guard where you place your affections, and how freely you allow your emotions to run. If someone is getting too close, it is our responsibility to put up the necessary barriers to intimacy. This may be anything from not taking phone calls; to referring them to another counselor; to having candid conversations (with your spouse present) to ensure that the message is clear.

A wise pastor will also give his wife the freedom to speak into his life, if she is uncomfortable with a situation. He should also adjust his boundaries so she feels secure. I am not sure why, but a wife has a special discernment for noticing these types of things. Maybe it's because we speak "girl." It is often obvious to us, before it is obvious to them. I don't know many husbands who regret having boundaries that were too tight; but I do know many men who live to regret not having boundaries that were not tight enough. Those men are usually divorced, or out of ministry now.

When You Lose a Close Friend in Ministry

This is one that has been particularly hard for me. Because of my mistrust of women over the years, I am pretty slow at developing friendships. I really stink at the superficial stuff in relationships, so it takes time for me to get close to someone. When I finally develop an authentic friendship, it is very important to me.

People leave the church. We all understand that. What we don't understand is how people that you spent so much time, energy, and joy with can suddenly walk away without realizing the pain it causes your heart. It is one of the worst kinds of betrayals. We even understand the cycles of ministries and we totally understand that people don't always fit your church's personality. But people that have been there with you through difficult times or supported, encouraged, or even proclaimed the vision that God has given—that is a tough hurt to deal with.

I am praying it doesn't happen to you too often. When it does, you must find the courage to process it and move forward. When your heart is too heavy, you will find that God will carry you through. Having walked through it, I see now that the pain eases (though it always hurts a bit), and life continues. The question of pivotal importance is what condition your heart will be in when you come through. You always have a choice. The most common response is to pull your heart in and refuse to take a risk again.

This is dangerous to you. It allows the enemy a stronghold in your heart that keeps you afflicted and controlled by him. Refuse to give him any territory in your anger. Refuse to be on his side in this process. Love must take risks and be vulnerable, if it is truly going to be called love. Love that takes no risks or makes no sacrifice is really not love at all. That's why it hurts so much.

But the worst thing you can do is close your heart off from loving the people who remain in front of you. In fact, it is usually through your choice to continue to risk loving and building new friendships that you find true healing and grace to move on. Go on gracefully, knowing that God will care for your battered heart. He is *for* your healing because it always points people back to Him when they look at you.

When a Staff Member Betrays You

It's not hard to understand what causes breakdown in ministry teams. Ministry is difficult, emotionally and personally taxing. Sometimes one, or both parties, refuse to deal properly with conflict, poor communication, negative interpretations, or misunderstandings. Sometimes it's just pride. You can't control everybody. Really, you can't control anybody. If you try, you will end up very frustrated and usually come out looking like a control freak.

I am a control freak without Jesus. My husband is the complete opposite. He is very comfortable just letting things play out. As you can imagine, we make each other crazy when we face situations like this. I think God was smart in putting us together. It keeps each of us from going off the deep end on either extreme, and forces us to find a healthy place in the middle.

When you hire someone to be on staff, you always take a risk. People have mastered the art of putting forward the best face on a resume, social media, or even in the interview. You can ask difficult questions, call references, but ultimately, you must be willing to take a risk when you hire someone. They also take a risk coming to work for you. Let me add, in most cases, you will end up with great staff. These instances of betrayal have been few and far between for us.

Nevertheless, it is a tense situation when a staff member rises up in opposition, or acts in a spirit of division. You must stay grounded as a leader and respond in a spirit of humility. You and your spouse will need to pray and plan how to deal with this situation in a godly way. You can't be afraid to deal with confrontation in ministry.

You may also have to put aside some of your own personal rights to protect your church. That can be hard for people because our hearts cry out for justice. Choose your battles carefully. If you are impulsive by nature, put boundaries in place to protect yourself and your church from reacting the wrong way. A good friend of mine once told me we have a choice: *respond or react.* A servant-leader will need to respond rather than react, to not only protect him, but also to protect the church.

As the spouse, you may be a target as well. It is important to plan out how you will respond, in the event it occurs. Proverbs warns us, often, of the dangers of reacting in anger. It takes more strength to be silent than it does to fly off the handle. Again, it is always about *what* is right in God's sight, not *who* is right. Jesus spent very little time defending Himself. He did not avoid the issues, but He continually led His followers. He did not cower away in hiding when people accused, or challenged Him.

Worse, probably, than overreacting, is avoidance. Our church needs to know that we can lead them during these difficult times and that we will lead them in doing the right thing. If you do not act decisively (not divisively), people will feel insecure about your leadership. Be that man or woman, and trust that God will care for and protect you.

In the unfair situations we faced, we found that submission to Christ always ensured God's favor and eventual, vindication. The proof is in the pudding. Jesus said, *"By their fruit you will recognize them...A good tree cannot bear bad fruit, and a bad tree cannot bear good fruit."* (Matt.7:16, 18) If the heart of your staff member is bad, it won't stay hidden forever. It just can't; God has a way of bringing the ugly things and *truth* to light.

Finally, I should mention that we live in a culture that loves to throw everything out on the table for everyone to judge, especially through social media. If you do this during your difficult situations, you're making bad trades. Is it worth it to be heard by the world, if it keeps people from coming to Christ? Passion for justice doesn't give us the right to stir the pot when it involves the hearts and souls of real people.

I believe that God will hold us accountable if we don't care for people above our need to justify ourselves. He is a just God, as well as a loving God, so we can trust Him with whatever situation we find ourselves in. In fact, it helps to understand this principle: *justice cannot exist without love, and love cannot be love without justice.* Real justice is only justice *if* driven by love. Real love only exists for the higher good (justice) of another. One, without the other, is really a counterfeit of both.

It is no good to claim that we are justified in causing division in the body of Christ merely for the sake of being right. We find the intersection of love and justice at the cross. If we are going to resemble Him, we should learn how that blending of justice and love works best. Follow the example of Christ and pick up your cross. Pick it up even when it is hard. Pick it up, *especially*, when it is hard. Trust God to be your Defender. Don't shrink back in fear or intimidation, but walk in courage bearing well the responsibility He has given you.

If you are faithful to do this, He will take care of your heart and wounded soul in every situation. Trust that He also has the right perspective and power to deal with mean-spirited or divisive people in your life.

He will always have the last word in every situation—always.

Chapter 12

Help! What Can I Do to Help My Wife?

This final chapter is for your husband. So many men really want to love their wives well, and see them thrive and grow to pour out great beauty upon their homes, church, and world. Unfortunately, so many really don't know where to begin and they fumble along doing the best they can.

I want to help you. Obviously, I don't have all the answers. I know women are a mystery at times! But I've been a woman a long time and I've been married for over twenty years while being in ministry. Most importantly, I've been fortunate enough to be married to a man who has spent our marriage pouring out his heart and life to give me the freedom to blossom. He has been patient and strong in those difficult times where I faltered. He has taught me well what it means for a man to love his wife like Christ has loved the church.

Pastor, your wife is your greatest ally in ministry. The time you take to care, protect, and provide an environment for her to blossom will pay great dividends—or not. If you neglect her, abuse her, or ridicule her, it will cost you and your church. As pastors, we must face this truth: *what we do in the dark matters.* What you say to her, what you pour into her, and what you invest into your marriage matters. What you think in your private thought life matters. What you view on the computer screen matters. It matters to your spiritual relationship with God. It matters to her spiritual relationship with God. It matters to your relationship to each other. It matters to your children. Finally, it matters to your church. No matter your charisma, good looks, eloquent teaching, or great leadership insight, if you are not careful in this area, it will discredit everything else. I cannot overstate this point.

Jesus says it best in Luke 6:41-42:

"Why do you look at the speck of sawdust in your brother's eye and pay no attention to the plank in your own eye? How can you say to your brother, 'Brother, let me take the speck out of your eye,' when you yourself fail to see the plank in your own eye? You hypocrite, first take the plank out of your eye, and then you will see clearly to remove the speck from your brother's eye."

I love that Jesus is direct. He doesn't beat around the bush, because He cares about how well you see, especially as a leader.

You must have clear vision if you are going to lead your church. If you want to teach them how to navigate life according to God's principles, you must live according to God's principles. We must continually guard against the idea that we have "arrived." Your care of your wife can be an ugly plank, or it can freely leave you with clear vision to lead others into a healthy understanding of what love, marriage, and selflessness looks like.

I believe it is one of the primary reason Paul likens marriage to the relationship of Christ with the church. If you can't love and lead your bride well, should you be leading *His* bride? These are hard words. It does not negate your wife's responsibility in how she responds and behaves, but I believe every pastor should understand the great gift they have in caring for God's daughter, especially in ministry.

Learning the Art of Blossoming

So how do you help your wife blossom? I believe it starts with understanding how a woman is wired. Many years ago, John and Stasi Eldredge wrote a couple of books that began to build a bridge between men and women, and how we see each other. From those books came the understanding of how men and women are wired—and oh, we are wired so very differently! Obviously, there are exceptions, and there is a continuum on the scale of those wirings.

But for the most part, a woman seeks to have two basic questions answered:

1. *Am I worthy to be loved?*
2. *Will I be safe?*

Some of the most critical mistakes men make in marriage come in answering these two questions with a negative, rather than an affirmative answer. So many men stop the pursuit and romance when they get married. That should be just the beginning of an exciting adventure of romance and intimacy as you get to know each other.

Instead, they walk around blindly, never understanding that their neglect is usually bringing out all the insecurities she has. Even worse, she may have completely shut down emotionally because she is tired of the fight to get her husband to really love her or be in her world.

I recently spoke to a woman who has essentially emotionally separated from her husband. When I asked her how he was handling it, she scoffed and answered, *"He thinks everything is just fine. He doesn't realize that it's over."* I began to wonder how a man could be so clueless. He had spent very little time making her feel that she was worthy of love. He also failed over and over to carry the load of ensuring she felt safe physically, financially, and emotionally. I looked at his life and what he was doing with it and realized he was so distracted by the pursuit of "things," that he wasn't in tune at all to the needs of his wife. I have no idea when his "AHA" moment will come. It will probably be when she hands him the divorce papers. By then, it is usually too late.

So how you are presently answering these two questions in your marriage? Do you know how your wife is wired to respond? Do you know if you are answering these questions at all? If you don't know, it's time to find out. It will hopefully bring great freedom and intimacy to your marriage.

Am I worthy to be loved? At first glance, this may seem like an easy question for you to answer. Of course, she is worthy to be loved! However, I think it's important to understand the pattern of negative thinking and embedding of insecurities that takes place in a woman's mind when she has been hurt emotionally.

The Heart of Insecurity

Let me start at the beginning, so this makes better sense. We first seek to have this question answered from the moment we are born. We ask our parents as infants. Most answer with a yes, and then they give us the love that we need to help us grow into securely, attached children. But, some parents don't. Some have ignored us, shamed us, or even abused us, until our hearts are deeply wounded. When this happens to a woman, she may spend an inordinate amount of time in life looking for someone, or something else, to help her answer this question because it was never answered with an affirmative as a child.

As we grow up as little girls, we, sometimes, look to our friends to affirm us, but how many friends can devote the time and energy it takes to answer this great of a question? We may chase after our quest for loveliness with the latest in beauty fads, shopping trips, or gym memberships. If we could just be beautiful, skinny, fashionable, popular, smart...enough—maybe then, we could feel loved? Unfortunately, those things are very temporary and we never feel loved for long, so we continue on our quest for anything to make us feel valuable.

As we grow into adolescence, we may turn to the opposite sex to answer this question. If the vacuum of our heart was never filled, this is usually the most dangerous time in our lives. We seek a man to give us hope that we are truly worth loving. Sometimes we uncover ourselves to draw in someone—*anyone*—to make us feel loved, even if it's only for a moment. We don't realize that when men truly value something, they cover it so it is cherished and protected.

By the time we enter marriage, we are often bitterly disappointed by our experiences and because there are few men who are willing to lay down their lives to love us unconditionally. Few men seem to know how to communicate love to us at all. Most simply use us for their own gratification, or worse, bully us around until we are more insecure—more fearful. Few men are willing to believe we are worth the time and commitment to show us real love and see the woman that we can become. So, unfortunately, our neediness grows.

Will I be safe? Obviously, if the first question was answered with a negative too often, a woman will not feel safe to love and blossom. Too many of us try to answer the question of safety for ourselves, and we do this, primarily, by control. Sometimes, this may refer to our physical safety; but most of the time it speaks of the emotional safety of loving someone. Obviously, if your wife is not physically safe in her relationship or home, this is a big problem.

But men can also do things that undermine the emotional safety of a woman, and it does something to a woman inside. When a woman offers her love to her spouse, and continually finds it rejected, or ignored (which she may still perceive as rejection), she may eventually stop offering. When her heart has been betrayed by her husband's time or attention to a thousand other loves besides hers, she will create thick walls around her heart.

Once a woman learns that she can't depend on her spouse (emotionally or financially), she has to figure it out on her own. Unfortunately, this usually makes for an angry or resentful spouse because she has to spend so much time and energy providing for that safety.

I understand this so well because, as I mentioned before, without Jesus, I am a control freak at heart. With Jesus, I am a control freak in rehab. I required a great deal of reassurance from my husband that I could let go of my need to control everything and find safety in our relationship, even in the little things. I feared so many things in those early years of marriage.

Some women fear being caged or trapped in a relationship. Others fear being pushed away. So we usually avoid those things that frighten us, like intimacy, vulnerability, or authenticity. If forced into a corner, we may "overreact," and all the while, we wonder if anyone understands what it feels like to feel so emotionally unsafe. This is a glimpse into the heart of insecurity.

Give God a Helping Hand

Obviously, God has answered both of these questions in the affirmative for every girl. He is the One who wired us to blossom with great beauty inside, but so many girls and women don't know that.

Even women who have been followers of Christ for some time may struggle to find their true identity and worth in Christ alone because they have been so badly beaten down and wounded by life. Sometimes the pain and disappointments of that life is so great that it leaves them closed up, believing that they are not worthy of love and able to safely open themselves up emotionally again. God laid down all of His life in love for each of us. He made us to live safely under His protective shelter, not in our emotionally guarded shell and He promises that He will never leave us or forsake us. It is the ultimate love story.

So many women spend their entire lives and never realize God was there all the time waiting for them to know Him. We, as women who follow Christ, need to learn to trust Him enough to step out and face our fears by hiding all of ourselves (insecurities and all) in Him.

However, husband, you must also understand that God brings people into our lives to lead us in this process. They can either help or hinder the process of making us more into the image of His Son. You, as a husband to His daughter, can work with God in this process. Allow me to explain.

Lessons from the Horse World

One of my greatest passions comes from working with horses. I spend a great deal of time practicing relational horsemanship techniques that teach people how to communicate with horses. The challenge, in natural horsemanship, is that all horses are uniquely wired, so what works for one horse, usually will not work for the next one. Working with different horses teaches you how to vary and improve your skills, and ultimately, set your horse up to succeed. It's always about putting the relationship with the horse *over* the task you want to accomplish.

You can probably imagine that this was a hard lesson for me to learn as a perfectionist, because I have a hard time getting my eyes off the end result. You, husband, may need to learn this, too. Learning these skills has taught me a great deal about my leadership style, and how I must learn better to deal with people, especially those closest to me.

You can tell a great deal about a horse by how they respond when they are frightened. I believe the same is true of women. Obviously, they are much smarter, more complex, and definitely, more beautiful than horses, but the similarities have been amazing to discover. We find that so many women benefit and grow emotionally through horse therapy and relational horsemanship for the primary reason of the emotional connections they have with our horses.

Some horses will fight, if backed into a corner. So will some women. Silencing or forcing your wife into submission may be a picture of emotionally backing her into a corner.

Some horses will flee if pushed into doing something that frightens them when they don't feel secure. You can cripple your wife emotionally if you push her to face her fear without gentleness and time.

Some horses work hard to keep from making a connection *(mostly those dominant mares)* with their handler because they are so against being led because of mistrust. There are women out there that need to feel respected and heard by their spouse, in order to be led so they can learn it is safe to trust.

Some horses will not stop moving long enough to engage you emotionally. It is safer to keep moving. For women, this translates to the "Martha" syndrome; a constant need to *do* in order to feel valuable.

If I work with an insecure horse and approach her with a great deal of energy and force, she usually reacts negatively. She may run away from me, explode, or stop listening. This is very dangerous for both of us because a frightened horse is a dangerous horse.

How true is this of women? I believe that women act out dangerously, hurt others, or simply turn off emotionally because they are afraid and insecure. The definition of insecure is: *unsafe, vulnerable, fearful, not confident.* All of us have some kind of insecurities or vulnerabilities. If every time a woman tries to communicate with you about her fear or vulnerability, she is met with force, apathy, ridicule, or intimidation, she will eventually stop trying.

Her emotional insecurities may not even have anything to do with you, but they will still linger from the baggage of the past. Regardless of where it comes from, God has placed you in her life to help provide a safe place of restoration that includes gentleness, love, and hope for something greater: *freedom to accept and love the woman that God made her to be.*

I remember a day when my husband was struggling greatly with my irrational fears and insecurities. He finally looked at me in desperation and said, *"You tell me what you want me to do to make you safe and comfortable and I will do it!"* Maybe he spoke it more out of frustration than love, but that didn't matter. It was a pivotal moment in my fearful heart when I realized the gift he was offering me: *the freedom to heal under his protection until I was no longer afraid, no matter how long it took.*

Suddenly the pressure was off and I could stop covering my fear (which I wasn't doing well anyway) and really start dealing with it.

He was learning how to set me up for success; learning what it looks like to blossom his wife.

"Husbands love your wives just as Christ loved the church..." (Eph. 5:25) Isn't this what God has asked all husbands to do? My heart breaks when I see an impatient or uncaring man messing up his marriage by refusing to love his wives patiently while she heals and grows.

Have you offered this to your wife? While you travel this road of ministry, there will be so many personal attacks on your wife. Even if she was a relatively secure woman when you married her, life and ministry rejection can take a toll on her. She is going to need your arms, your ear, and your reassurance as she deals with all that your ministry journey together will bring her.

The benefits will outweigh the cost— if you choose to partner with God in this! Invest the time in getting to know and understand her. Choose to blossom her by listening (not fixing) and affirming her in whatever she feels God is calling her to do. Work *with* God in this blossoming process. Love her patiently, respecting her fearful insecurities with no strings attached. Refuse to crush her with harsh words, or negligence, or bully her with ridicule or intimidation. Love always protects. Guard fiercely the place around her heart from the enemy, and from cruel people. Remind her again and again that you, like her Christ, will love her, even if she stumbles. Communicate that she can be safe with you and that you will wait as long as it takes until she is no longer afraid.

When you answer both of her core questions with an affirming "yes," you help her find safety in your love to believe and trust again. This was and is *still* the greatest gift my husband has ever given me since that day so many years ago. He is my biggest fan and our maturing love is greater than anything we experienced in those early days of marriage.

There is another kind of horse. She is a left-brained mare and is not insecure. She is self-assured, confident, and sometimes, quite opinionated. She needs a leader. But her leader must be one that earns her respect. A leader who backs her into the corner will find that she comes out fighting. She will not stand to being forced. However, if her leader is too timid or complacent, she will take over the leadership.

God has placed us equal in value, but with different roles in the marriage. A two-headed creature is a monster. So is a two-headed household. Both men and women are strong, but they were called to fight and work *together*, not against each other over control of the home. I understand what the culture tells you, and I understand that sometimes the church messed up what it told you in the past. Yet, neither of these negates the God-given design laid out for men and women, or how the home should operate.

We live in a day where women are strong and self-supporting, at least in the United States. It is easy for them to take over the leadership role that God set up. Some women do it, because they believe they can do it better. Others do it because husbands have "checked-out" of the leadership of their home. Perhaps he has done this because it was too much work to lead or cast a vision. Whatever the reason, things are mixed up, and where there is leadership confusion, there is disunity. Take the time to get your marriage reorganized and aligned. God didn't set it up to make you all miserable, but to help you both become the son and daughter He sees you to be.

Throughout history, the Christian world has also seen a great abuse of the "roles" God ordained for men and women. Men, sometimes, demanded the absolute submission of women, without the mutual offering of love and sacrifice for her as Christ gave the church.

Why would she give away something so powerful and precious when it would not be cherished? You see, submission cannot be demanded, it must be offered. You can force me physically, emotionally, or maybe even verbally, but you can never conquer my heart. I must offer it to you. Too many men have *demanded* that which was created and designed to be *offered* in love and respect.

Additionally, a woman was not made to be merely a companion. Adam had companionship in the animals. He needed help. God said it was *not good* that he was alone. Help for Adam came in the form of Eve. She brought completeness to the family. It was the reality of "one flesh" not just physically, but spiritually, and emotionally, as well.

The moment we stop legalistically defining submission, is the moment we will find the true freedom and beauty in it. It is a gift I give my husband, but it is not really about my husband at all. I do it because God has asked me to and I see it as worship unto Him. I choose not to be subordinate, but to come together with my husband and be likeminded (freely offering my gifts in the vision) in our family vision. How can it not mirror Christ and the church when we both submit under God?

Pastor, you *can* lead your wife well.

Pastor's wife, God *can* help you be an amazing leader and source of inspiration to prosper your family *and* enjoy your life in ministry.

It will be a refining journey for both of you, but I know it will also be a worthwhile journey that brings a great joy and a great harvest not only to your church, but also to the generations of your family.

I pray for both of you. I pray that your love for each other, and for Christ, will only grow deeper each day that you serve together.

I pray for your church. I pray that they will come to know Christ more intimately because of your leadership and influence. I pray that they will be better men and women of God because of the opportunities you take to serve as a couple together as ministers. You have this moment. You have this time in which God has placed you to lead and to love your church and pour out your gifts together upon His Bride.

Do it well.

About the Author

Kimberly Waldie is married to her best friend, mother to four great (and challenging) kids, and pastor's wife to an awesome church in Traverse City, MI. She has served over 22 years in ministry to children, youth, women, and currently, alongside her husband, as lead pastors. She has a passion for speaking, teaching, and mentoring people to discover their true identity in Christ and navigate the challenges of life. She graduated with a Bachelor's Degree in Social Work from Ferris State University. As a social worker and adoptive mom, she has worked with families in the realm of foster care and adoption. She enjoys riding her horses, using them in ministry, writing, and spending time outside with her family. Find more of her writings and blog posts at: **http://lifeinthecrashlane.wordpress.com**